7/10

THE
250
QUESTIONS
EVERY
LANDLORD
SHOULD ASK

D0062270

George Sheldon

NRC   CASS COUNTY PUBLIC LIBRARY
400 E. MECHANIC
HARRISONVILLE, MO 64701

BUSINESS

Avon, Massachusetts

0 0022 0360182 4

Copyright © 2009 by F+W Media, Inc.
All rights reserved. This book, or parts thereof, may not be reproduced in any
form without permission from the publisher; exceptions are made for brief
excerpts used in published reviews.

Published by Adams Business
An imprint of Adams Media, a division of F+W Media, Inc.
57 Littlefield Street, Avon, MA 02322. U.S.A.
www.adamsmedia.com

ISBN 10: 1-59869-832-X
ISBN 13: 978-1-59869-832-9

Printed in the United States of America.

J I H G F E D C B A

Library of Congress Cataloging-in-Publication Data
is available from the publisher.

This publication is designed to provide accurate and authoritative information
with regard to the subject matter covered. It is sold with the understanding
that the publisher is not engaged in rendering legal, accounting, or other professional advice. If legal advice or other expert assistance is required, the services of a competent professional person should be sought.
   —From a *Declaration of Principles* jointly adopted by a Committee of the
American Bar Association and a Committee of Publishers and Associations

Many of the designations used by manufacturers and sellers to distinguish
their products are claimed as trademarks. Where those designations appear in
this book and Adams Media was aware of a trademark claim, the designations
have been printed with initial capital letters.

This book is available at quantity discounts for bulk purchases.
For information, call 1-800-289-0963.

CONTENTS

ACKNOWLEDGMENTS

This is my thirty-first published book. There are so many people for me to thank: from my mentor, the late Charles W. Byrd of Hershey, PA, to my agent Bob Diforio. Both have provided unwavering support and advice the entire time I have known them.

Special thanks to Peter Archer at Adams Media. He always believed in my ability to produce this book. I want to thank everyone else at Adams Media that worked on this book, too. From the copyeditor Mark Sehestedt to the page layout artists, from the indexer to the cover designer, I appreciate your hard work and efforts, which have made this work as good as it could be. I very much appreciate everything you have done.

George Sheldon
Lancaster, PA
(*www.georgesheldon.com*)

DEDICATION

This one is for Reagan S. Sheldon, another fine grandson.

INTRODUCTION

Becoming a landlord is an exciting experience that can be profitable, wonderful, and mind-boggling. The decision to become a landlord soon becomes a process. There are many things to learn as you take the big step into real estate investing and many things to do as you work with people and property. Solving problems is a primary task for you as a landlord. *The 250 Questions Every Landlord Should Ask* will guide you into the process of becoming a landlord and give you lots of advice in making your operation more profitable. There are five sections in this book, each one written to get you through the various stages of becoming a landlord. From evaluating the risks of becoming a landlord to learning how to get a coin-operated laundry on your rental property, this book will guide you through the steps, A to Z.

PART 1

Ideal (And Not So Ideal) Properties

YOU HAVE BEEN contemplating becoming a landlord. But where do you start? Before you can rent to a tenant, you need a property. There are good—and not so good—properties. This section will help you understand what types of properties make the best rentals. It will take you through the pros and cons of renting specific types of properties to tenants.

#1.   **What are some of the risks of being a landlord?**

Unfortunately, there are risks in owning property and renting it. Some of the risks are large, and others are small. Proper ownership, good management, and common sense can minimize many of them.

Perhaps the biggest risk is the loss of your investment. If you have a property worth $300,000, you could lose the equity in any number of ways. You could foolishly not maintain property insurance. A devastating fire could reduce your property to little more than smoldering ashes. This risk is easily avoided if you properly insure your property.

Other risks require good organizational skills on your part. Pay your taxes, or you run the risk of having the property taken away from you. Keeping track of rent payments is easy, but it must be done. You must properly maintain your property, keeping the premises in reasonable repair.

Another risk is that you could break a law and find yourself in big trouble. Some laws are designed to provide severe penalties to landlords. While you might not intentionally break a law, it is possible to face both civil and criminal penalties.

#2.   **Is being a landlord a good financial strategy?**

Most likely, it is. Being a landlord involves owning real estate as an investment. This offers a unique financial situation for the landlord.

Real estate is different from any other kind of investment. You can touch, feel, and use real estate. You cannot do that with a paper certificate that says you own stocks or bonds.

Real estate is the only investment where you can easily borrow funds to acquire it. Consider the purchase of a $100,000 investment property. With a down payment, it is easy to purchase the property. Asking a bank for the money is routine. Now consider asking the same bank to borrow money to purchase stocks or bonds. Your request will be both quickly and flatly denied.

As a landlord, your tenants will pay for the property for you. Each rent payment you receive allows you to recover your investment in the property. Whether you paid cash for the property or purchased it by acquiring financing, your tenant's rent allows you to recover your investment.

There are also substantial tax benefits when you own real estate as investment property.

#3.   Can I really make money as a landlord?

Some people make vast fortunes as landlords. Others earn modest fortunes, while others make little. There are no guarantees when you are a property owner. Collecting monthly rent from someone that wants to use your property is a sound and practical business. The issue is that you must have an active (and not passive) participation in the property.

As with any business, you must keep a careful watch over your expenses and your income. When something goes wrong, you must fix the problem. If a tenant stops paying rent, you must correct the problem to keep your income current. If expenses become too high, your profit dwindles.

With positive cash flow, a rental property becomes a true asset. Each year, the property appreciates. If you have a mortgage, the tenant provides the money you need to make your payment. In effect, your tenant is paying off your loan for you.

Consider the basics of rental property income: a property that produces $200 per month in positive cash flow creates $2,400 of yearly income. That may not sound like much, but consider the appreciation factor and that each month your equity increases as you pay down your loan. Each month, you owe less on the mortgage, your property value increases, and your equity grows.

#4.   Is there really a demand for rental properties?

Yes. People always need a place to live. Statistics change, but generally speaking, about one-third of the population lives in rental property. According to the U.S. Census Bureau, about 30 percent of Americans rent rather than own their homes. There always seems to be a healthy demand for rental units.

The local economy often affects the current need for rental property. When employment is good, people need housing near their jobs. This is especially true when local employers seek employees from out of the area. Support industries (health care, transportation, or retail, for example) to the local employers also can create rental-housing demands.

Lower regional unemployment often increases the demand for rental units. That is because people are moving into the area for jobs and income. When jobs are lost, people tend to move away, and the demand for rental property can decrease. Any area where the local economy is doing well is always a good place for landlords to own property.

As long as people change jobs, marry, divorce, move, have children, make more or less money, or have any other life changing events, you can be assured there will be a need for rental property. The demand can increase and decrease, but there is always a need.

#5.   Is being a landlord difficult?

It depends on what "difficult" means to you. Real estate, as an investment, is different from paper securities. If you were to invest $100,000 in stocks, your investment exists only on a paper certificate. To the contrary, an investment in real estate is something you can see, touch, and behold.

That also means that real estate needs care and maintenance. Parts of ownership include cleaning, repairing, fixing, and replacing.

Add to the mix of items that you must carefully watch are your tenants. Most tenants will become good customers. The majority will pay their rent, treat your property almost as if it were their own, and will, by paying their rent, make you money.

It's up to you to whom you rent your property, just as the decisions regarding maintenance and repairs are yours. What you do—and what you do not do—can make your life as a landlord "difficult" and filled with stress, or not. You need to deal with people, make sound decisions, and take care of little problems before they become large and uncontrollable.

#6. How much work is involved in owning properties?

The work depends on the type of property, its condition, and the tenants that you acquire.

Obviously, a property with one rental unit (a single-family residence) and a property with multiple rental units present different challenges and requirements. Single-family residences, for example, have only one heating unit to maintain. Multiple-family properties often have multiple heating units and multiple bathrooms. In other words, properties with multiple mechanical units require more work to maintain them.

The condition of the property often determines the amount of work required. A property that has been well maintained is likely to require less work than one that has been abused or mistreated. Maintenance and minor fixes prevent costly repairs. Problems that have not been resolved often make additional work for the property owner. For example, a toilet that has not been repaired can cause work and ongoing problems for the landlord—a slow drip from the input pipe can damage the floorboards and the ceiling, as well as being the catalyst for rot and mold. The tenants need to use the toilet, so fix it right away. Not taking care of a reported leak can turn a simple, inexpensive repair into a costly one.

The total amount of work is often determined by the general condition of the property and the tenants. Often the difference between a profitable or disastrous investment is the amount of work an investor is willing to put into their rental property. Not everyone is willing to screen tenants, track down overdue rents, or respond to middle-of-the-night repair messages.

#7.   What are some of the common problems many landlords experience?

Complying with the various laws and finding good tenants are the most common problems most landlords encounter.

Too many landlords get themselves in legal trouble. It may not be intentional, but it happens often. Many regulations, ordinances, and laws must be followed. Violations can range from warnings to fines and imprisonment. One of the problems is that local laws vary so much between jurisdictions. In one locality, a landlord may be required to supply a working smoke detector. In another municipality, there are no requirements. Another local jurisdiction may require both a smoke detector and a fire extinguisher be installed in every rental unit.

Landlords seem to agree that their biggest problem is finding good tenants. This can always be a challenge. Fear of loss of rental income often results in landlords accepting tenants that they should not. As a landlord, your main objective is to find and keep good, problem-free tenants.

#8.   What is the best type of property to use for rental income?

The best property type is one that will produce positive cash flow for the landlord. It does not matter if the property is a single-family residence, a multiple-family residence (such as an apartment building), a commercial building, or any other property type. What matters is that someone else will pay you for the use of the real estate.

Farmland is often rented by the owner to a farmer who uses it to produce crops. Undeveloped commercial property is often rented for storage use. Some sell monthly lot rents, such as a mobile home park. The possibilities of creating rental income are endless.

Real estate that provides housing produces rental income. Some properties are more fitted for housing rental than others. For example, properties located in high crime areas are not going to generate the same income as a property located on a lake in a pastoral setting.

Some properties will attract certain types of tenants. A three-bedroom property is likely to attract a family with children. A one-bedroom property is likely to attract tenants without children. In reality, just about any property can produce rental income.

#9.   How much should I pay for a rental property?

The answer to this question can be both easy and complicated. The easy answer is to pay as little as possible. Many real estate experts say that you make your money when you buy the property. So getting it for the right price is fundamental.

However, the property must be able to generate a positive cash flow. If you are paying cash for the property and not financing the purchase, any rental income above the fixed annual costs (taxes, insurance, etc.) would create positive cash flow. When financing is involved, the rental income must be above the monthly loan payment. If the loan payment is $1,200, the amount of rent must be more. If not, the property is not a good rental property unless you can borrow less money to reduce the monthly payment to be below the property's rental income.

Locating properties that can produce reasonable income is not impossible, but it does take some work. Consider the purchase price as a large part of the why you should purchase or pass on a potential income producing property.

#10. Are there any types of properties that I should avoid?

The properties to avoid are those that are difficult to rent. For example, you may find a great deal on a townhouse. However, the property on one side is a boarded-up, burned-out shell. On the other side, the property is dilapidated and condemned. If you were to rent it, the amount of rent you could reasonably expect to collect would be less than if the adjoining properties were in reasonably good shape.

Curb appeal is just one of the many factors potential tenants will use to select the places they want to use as their homes. Real estate that does not offer basic appeal is not a good rental income-producing property.

The other kinds of properties to avoid are those that have expensive problems that need immediate attention. A property with foundation problems can become a money pit. There could be extensive water damage, rot, and other structural issues that need to be fixed to prevent future problems.

#11. What is the most I should pay for a rental property?

There is no limit as to the maximum that you should pay to purchase a rental property. Any type of property can produce rental income.

Some properties cost most than others, and that is usually due to the location. A property in one location compared to a similar property in another could cost tens of thousands of dollars more or less.

There is no set rule as to the maximum you should pay for a rental. However, you must be realistic about the cost of the property versus the amount of monthly rent you can reasonably expect to collect. For example, a property that could only generate $500 of rental income is not worth $500,000 to purchase it. The property may be worth $500,000 (or even more) because of its potential or location, but as a rental income property, it does not generate sufficient income to cover expenses and the investment.

Experienced landlords use different methods or formulas of determining what they are willing to pay for a property. Some of these techniques are:

- Do not buy the property if it costs more than 100 times the rental income (if the property produces $1,000 of rent, the purchase price is $100,000).
- Pay only 70 to 75 percent of the property's value.

Because real estate markets vary so much locally, these particular formulas may need to be adjusted for your area.

#12. Do fixer-uppers make the best rental investment properties?

Fixer-uppers are those properties that need major repairs or renovations. The current owner, for whatever reason, did not maintain the property. Sometimes called ugly houses, fixer-uppers may require a little or a lot of work to make them habitable and rentable.

A fixer-upper can be an excellent rent-producing property. The issue is always how much time and money it will take to rehabilitate the property. The cost of the acquisition of the property, added with the cost of repairs, determines the total investment. The reason fixer-uppers are often sought is that they can be acquired for below market value. Even with the repair or rehab cost, the total investment can be significantly less than a similar property.

Many successful landlords that invest in fixer-upper properties often do some—if not most—of the rehabilitation themselves. It is not uncommon for the landlord to complete the simpler, less complicated do-it-yourself repairs, which include minor plumbing, carpentry, and other small projects. Major repairs, such as replacing the roof or installing a new furnace are usually contracted with a local company.

The fixer-upper may need cosmetic repairs, including painting, new carpeting, or flooring. Landscaping, new windows, and updated appliances can often greatly change the appearance of a property.

#13.   How do I find good rental properties?

There is no single way to find a rental property. Successful landlords employ various methods to locate potential investment properties.

Most landlords are always on the lookout for good rental properties. They read the classified real estate advertisements. They look for real estate "For Sale" signs in neighborhoods where they want to own property. They usually ask a real estate agent to look for potential properties in the local multilist system. They search the Internet.

Successful landlords also watch foreclosure lists for potential rental properties. Properties in foreclosure are often acquired below market value and are converted to rental units. Some investors purchase the property from the distressed homeowner and then rent it back to them. Sometimes this strategy works, but if the homeowner could not make the mortgage payment, it is unlikely he can make the rent payment.

Another source are local properties that are currently for rent. Aggressive investors call landlords that are trying to rent their property and inquire if the property might be for sale. Landlords tired of the maintenance, tenant turnovers, and managing the property are often willing to sell their investment property.

#14.   Do starter properties make better rental properties?

Starter homes (the types of properties that are often called first-time homebuyer houses) can become great rental properties. There are several reasons why:

- *Price:* They cost less. One of the reasons they are starter homes is because of their lower asking price.
- *Basic property:* These are properties that provide the basics, without many frills. This means there are fewer things to maintain.
- *Lower rent:* Since the property costs less to acquire and maintain, tenants can be charged less rent and the landlord can still make money.
- *Higher demand:* Basic, lower-priced rental properties are always in demand. It is easier to rent and retain tenants in a property where the rent is lower.
- *Easy disposal:* Should the property need to be sold, it is often easier to sell because the asking price is lower. There just seems to be more buyers for a starter home.

This doesn't mean that other properties can't be good moneymaking rental units. It just seems that starter homes are preferred by many successful landlords.

#15. Should I buy properties that are already being used as rental properties?

The main advantage of purchasing a property that is already a rental property is that you can review its financial records. This allows you to judge the profitability of the property.

You can examine the income and expenses. You can see what the record of accomplishment of rents collected has been. You can also see what it costs to maintain and operate the property. By adding in your financing costs (if any), you can determine if the property could provide monthly income.

Owners of rental properties must maintain records for tax purposes. These records are not complicated and are easily compiled by the property owner. A landlord will often make them available for serious buyers. Property owners that are not current landlords are less likely to be able to provide detailed operating costs. From the landlord's current financial records, you can examine how well the property has been maintained and what future repairs are likely to be needed. Don't overlook how valuable this information can be in determining future costs.

One other advantage is that the rental property often comes with a tenant that is paying rent. While you did not select the tenant, your renter will continue to pay rent when you assume ownership of the property.

#16. How much should I spend to convert a property to one that produces rental income?

You should spend what you can recover within a two-year period. If the conversion cannot be covered within two years, then the property probably cannot be profitably acquired and converted.

Ideally, of course, you should spend as little as possible. Part of the costs will be determined by what local building codes, laws, and regulations require.

You might acquire a property that you intend to rent, and your only costs might be to add smoke detectors. After purchasing them at your local hardware store, you quickly install them yourself. So the conversion cost very little.

Another property might require installation of separate electrical service and meters to the two rental units. This work by a licensed electrician costs approximately $2,500. Over a two-year period, you can assume that it cost approximately $100 per month for the new wiring. (Two years is always a good measure of time to amortize acquisition costs.)

#17. How do I know a good deal when I see it?

A deal is one that you can acquire and make money by owning the property. Successful landlords are always looking for profitable properties to acquire. They will pass on many, just because there is something not right. It could be the timing, the price, the condition, or the location. There are numbers of reasons why they don't proceed with a purchase.

However, when they find a property that piques their interest, it is always because it is a good deal. The numbers make sense when analyzed. It is a property that will produce a positive cash flow.

Successful landlords don't fall in love with the property, but instead fall in love with the deal. If any property doesn't have the potential of creating positive cash flow, pass on it. The more money you can put down, the more profitable a property can be.

Calculate the potential of any possible rental property. Pass on any property where you cannot earn a monthly profit.

#18. Are multiple-family properties a better investment than single-family properties?

For long-term rental income investments, they often are. Properties that are designed to provide housing for more than one family (two units, three units, etc., or apartment houses) often can generate more income. For that reason, the additional income often makes these multifamily units quite attractive to landlords and real estate investors.

Consider a single-family property that you could purchase for $125,000 and would rent for $1,250 per month, and your positive cash flow is $250. Compare that to a two unit (two apartments) that you could purchase for the same $125,000. Each unit pays $800 in rent. Your monthly income is $1,600 ($800 × 2). Even if your expenses were higher, let's say $1,100, you are still ahead in monthly profit compared to the single-family unit. You received $1,600 in rent, less $1,100 in expenses, for a net of $500. That's $250 more per month, or $3,000 per year.

#19.   **Are two-family properties better or worse than three- or four-unit properties?**

Each property should be judged for its ability to produce a profitable monthly cash flow for you. Overall, the properties with more units are often more attractive to landlords. That's simply because the amount of money the property will generate each month is larger than a single-family unit. It's all about the cash flow.

Most successful landlords start out small and grow their real estate holdings. They start with one single-family (or a two-family) and go forward from that humble beginning. As they get more experience and knowledge, they move on to improved properties. As they continue to grow, they often acquire multifamily properties because it makes financial sense to do so.

Five (or more) rental units automatically classify the property as "investment" real estate under the guidelines for most loan programs. Most lenders package the loans in groups. The lenders sell the loan on the secondary mortgage market to investors. The lending rules state that any property over four units cannot obtain owner-occupant financing, even if the owner lives in one of the units. Five units and higher classify the property as strictly for "investment." This makes larger family units more difficult to sell because of financing restrictions. Properties with two to four units are often the ones more desirable to landlords.

#20.   **What are some of the financing options for acquiring rental investment properties?**

There are many different ways to finance investment properties. Traditional lenders (such as banks and private mortgage companies) offer various loan programs. There are also some government programs available to use.

When seeking financing, there are some fundamental points to consider:

- Never lie or be deceitful when applying for a loan. It is not only unethical, it is illegal. You could be prosecuted and sent to prison for lying on a loan application.
- Only seek the financing you need. Don't borrow more than you must.
- Shop around. Loan programs vary greatly from one lender to another. Just because one bank does not have a program you need, that doesn't mean it is unavailable from another.
- Costs matter. Analyze all loan programs before applying. Consider not only the interest rate, but also the loan's closing costs and fees.
- Down payment required. The down payment is something you must pay. Some programs will require little down, while others might require 25 to 30 percent of the selling price.

Your financing options will vary between lenders. Loan officers will gladly discuss their lender's options, and provide you with various ways that you might finance an investment property.

#21. How much money do I need for a down payment?

The amount of money you will need for a down payment will depend on several factors. They include the price of the property, the loan program, and the lender's requirement. Often lenders require larger down payments on non-owner-occupied (NOO) properties than they do for owner-occupied (OO) properties. Their reasoning is simple: a primary residence is less likely to be abandoned by the borrower. It is easier for an investor to walk away from an investment property. For that reason, they want to see a larger down payment from the borrower.

Many times, investors want to put the least amount down as possible, preferring to hold on to their cash. There is nothing wrong with this technique, as long as the property can generate positive cash flow.

Some try to buy investment property under cloudy (or even illegal) terms. For example, a $200,000 property is sold for $250,000. The buyer and seller agree to a "throwaway" second mortgage of $50,000. They tell the lender that there will be a $250,000 sale, with a $50,000 second mortgage, and seek a $200,000 loan. Hiding the material fact that the $50,000 second mortgage is nothing but a ruse to prevent a down payment is illegal.

The amount of down payment you will need will depend on the lender's loan criteria and requirements. Different rates and costs are often determined by the amount of the down payment.

#22.   **What is LTV?**

In real estate financing, there is a term known as Loan-to-Value ratio. It is often called LTV. This ratio compares the total of the loan to the value of the property. For example, a $150,000 loan on a $200,000 property is a 75 percent Loan to Value (LTV); this ratio shows the loan to the actual value of the real estate.

Real estate professionals may also use the term TLTV, or Total-Loan-to-Value-ratio. This is used when additional debts, such as a second or even a third mortgage, are secured by the property. For example, if there is a first mortgage on a $300,000 property of $200,000, and a second mortgage of $25,000, the TLTV is 75 percent ($200,000 first mortgage plus $25,000 second mortgage equals $225,000 divided by the fair market value of $300,000 = 75 percent).

A property with a lower LTV is always a more appealing loan. Lenders know that the higher the equity, the more likely their investment in the property is protected.

#23.   **Is it possible to acquire properties with no-money-down financing?**

Yes. It is quite possible to purchase rental properties without any down payment. It is not likely, but it is possible.

The owner of the property, for example, could agree to finance the property. If they own the property free and clear, they can do whatever they want. They can, for example, sell it to you for an agreed upon price, and give you a mortgage to pay off the property. Most people selling a property want the money right away and won't agree to a payment plan. Nevertheless, you could purchase a rental property with no money down this way.

Another way is to use a special loan program from a lender. Some lenders have offered programs where you take out two loans: one for 80 percent of the purchase price, and a second mortgage for the remaining 20 percent. The second mortgage is more risky for the lender, and a higher interest rate is charged.

Some government programs allow 100 percent financing if you will be living in one of the units. For example, if you are purchasing a four-unit property, you could acquire 100 percent financing if you will be living in one of the four units.

#24. **What is wrong with 100 percent financing?**

There is nothing wrong with buying real estate with no down payment. It is legal. It is not unethical.

The federal government has two programs where they offer 100 percent financing on real estate purchases. The Veterans Administration guarantees 100 percent financing to veterans buying a home. The United States Department of Agriculture also offers 100 percent financing through its rural housing program.

Some private lenders also offer 100 percent financing programs. Mortgage lenders often offer zero-down loans. Their 100 percent financing is available for applicants with good credit. Some lenders offer an 80 percent first mortgage and a 20 percent second mortgage, which combined provides 100 percent financing.

Financing 100 percent of the real estate purchase price is not impossible or illegal. Many lenders are ready to assist you to do so if the property is your primary residence. Properties not used as your primary residence are called non-owner-occupied (NOO). It is these properties—the type real estate investors acquire—where 100 percent financing is often not available.

#25. Are there any government programs that can help me become a landlord?

There is no simple, one-stop shop in the government that allows you to become a landlord quickly and easily. There is no single agency or bureau that openly lends money to someone that decides they want to become a real estate investor and collect rent from renters.

In the maze of government, however, there are different programs that might assist you in your goals. Regulations and rules change, but the U.S. Department of Housing and Urban Development (HUD) sometimes offers loan guarantee programs through the Federal Housing Agency (FHA). These programs permit the financing of repairs and the acquisition of the property. The loan is not made from the agency, but rather is guaranteed through an approved lender. You may need to contact several lenders until you get the information you need. Not all loan officers have training to offer these programs.

Sometimes states or local municipalities will offer programs that you can use. Some offer abandoned properties that they will sell at reduced prices to investors. This gets the dilapidated property back on the tax rolls.

#26. Should I use a mortgage broker to help find financing?

A mortgage broker is a person or company that specializes in mortgage loan originations and receives a commission for matching the borrower with a lender. The mortgage broker usually performs some or most of the loan processing functions such as taking a loan application, ordering a credit report, appraisal, and title report. The mortgage broker does not underwrite the loan and does not use his or her own money to fund the loan.

Borrowers with damaged or imperfect credit, or those needing financing for nontraditional properties, turn to the mortgage broker to help them find a loan. Because a broker has multiple contacts with many different lenders, the broker can usually find a loan program for the borrower. This is especially true for the landlord that needs a non-owner-occupied loan. Brokers have also found a niche in matching certain property types with lenders.

#27. Should I convert my current home into a rental unit?

Many of today's landlords started by converting their residence into a rental unit. It is not unusual that it was their first home.

There are often tax complications when you convert a private residence to an income producing property (and vice versa). The tax laws and regulations also change. Don't attempt to handle this part of the conversion yourself. Always seek the services of a tax professional whenever you are facing a complicated transaction. While you are not transferring the property to someone else, in the eyes of the taxing authority, you are moving the property into a completely new category. Previous deductions or exemptions may become voided when the property's designation is changed from primary residence to income producing.

Frequently the first property is refinanced. Cash is pulled out and used to acquire a new home. After a new primary residence is acquired, the first property, with the new financing in place, is then rented.

Of course, any current residence can be converted into a rental property (provided there are no deed restrictions or covenants prohibiting it). As long as the property can produce a positive monthly cash flow, it can work as a rental property.

#28.   **Are properties that have more than four units harder to finance?**

Multifamily properties that have more than four units are not impossible to finance, but the process is different. Fewer lenders actively seek these types of loans. That's because of Wall Street's control of housing loans and the packaging of the loans later to investors.

However, this does not mean that you cannot obtain financing for properties that have five or more rental units. But you should anticipate a different process than other real estate loans when applying for the loan.

Before seeking the financing, you should meet with your certified public accountant (CPA) and prepare a current financial statement. Although you could prepare the statement yourself, it will carry more weight if a CPA prepares it.

You will need to have the down payment funds available, as well as the closing costs. Be prepared to show proof that you do have the ability to make your down payment at the closing or settlement.

The lender is going to want to see sufficient income from the property to make the loan payments, as well as pay the operating expenses. If the property appraisal justifies the value, you should have no difficulty acquiring the loan.

#29.   **Do condos or co-ops make better rental units?**

Condominiums (commonly called condos) or building cooperatives (commonly called co-ops) do not necessarily make better rental units. Their main advantage is that exterior maintenance is done for you. You do not need to worry about how the grass will be cut or who will be clearing snow from the sidewalks. This type of property allows you to live worry-free of exterior maintenance. As a landlord, this can take away many of your property management concerns.

One consideration is what is included in the monthly fee. There are no set conditions or terms, so what is paid for can vary from property to property. Water, sewer service, and trash may be included, or they may not. Maintenance of common areas is typically covered.

Another factor to consider is the amount of funds on deposit for major capital expenditures. Is there enough money on deposit for roof repair or repaving of parking lots? Condominiums and co-ops that are underfunded could be forced to raise the condo fees to the unit owners to pay for necessary repairs and maintenance.

#30. **Are there any restrictions to renting a condo or co-op?**

There could be. It depends on the condo or co-op.

Before purchasing a condo or co-op for a rental property, you must determine if you have the right to rent your unit to a tenant. You might (or might not) be able to do so.

If you are permitted to rent your unit, you may need to have your tenant approved by a board before your potential tenant can move into the building. Each condo or co-op has its own rules, regulations, or covenants. Check them out carefully before purchasing the property.

Also, be aware that a rule could be passed that would eliminate renters (if they are permitted now). You need to monitor this closely. You cannot just sit back and not monitor what the condo or co-op board is doing. You must maintain contact and attend the meetings. If you do not, you could find yourself owning a rental income property that you cannot rent. If this happens, you can only sell the property and move on to another investment. However, if it does happen, you cannot sell it to another potential landlord because they cannot rent the property either.

#31. **What kinds of properties are best to avoid?**

There are several kinds of properties that landlords should not consider for renting. The most obvious type of property to avoid is one that is not capable of producing a positive monthly cash flow for the landlord. Do not invest in properties that can only produce negative cash flow each month. Move on to another potential investment rather than purchasing one that will cost you money each month.

Don't invest in properties that have undeterminable expenses or costs forthcoming. For example, suppose a local municipality has announced that a new sewer line will be constructed in front of a property you are considering buying. There is no way you can know the exact cost of the installation. The connection from the house could be simple, or it could become quite expensive if large rocks need to be removed. Unknown costs can turn a profitable property into a costly and unprofitable investment.

Also, avoid properties that are likely to be difficult to rent. Because of location or other factors, some properties are not going to be easy to find renters. Consider what you would need to collect, and ask if that monthly amount is likely to be paid by a potential renter for the property.

#32. Does it ever make sense to invest in a rental property that will produce only a negative cash flow?

Probably not. Negative cash flow is just that: each month there is not enough money generated by the rent. It costs you money each month.

If it is just a few dollars negative, and if you can raise rents soon, you could turn a negative cash flow property into a positive. In that situation, the purchase of a negative cash flow property may make sense.

Sometimes properties are underutilized, and that causes the negative cash flow situation. An example might be a property with two large bedrooms. By installing a partition in one of the bedrooms, the property is converted from a two-bedroom to a three-bedroom unit. Now a three-bedroom unit, the new higher rent changes it from a negative to a positive cash flow property.

Some successful landlords use this strategy exclusively when searching for properties to acquire. They only seek properties that are easily changed or modified so that higher rents can be collected. Modifications are not limited to just adding additional bedrooms. Updating kitchens and baths, adding a family room or playroom, or providing new appliances can often justify higher rents and turn a property into a positive cash flow.

#33. Are there any particular locations that attract tenants?

The location of your rental property is going to play a factor in your success as a landlord.

Properties located near schools, parks, shopping areas, transportation, and highways are those most desirable to potential tenants. Neighborhoods are also a prime consideration to renters. Some of the criteria are nothing more than personal opinion. For example, every local public school has its supporters and its critics.

Investing in what is considered good neighborhoods is usually the safest. Of course, it varies from one person to another as to what a good neighborhood is. Some people prefer off street parking, while others do not care. Some people consider mass transit an important asset to a property. The location of the property often determines what services or conveniences are nearby.

On the other side of the spectrum are those that prefer to be far from the bustle of communities. They prefer a rural location and do not mind a longer daily commute.

#34. What kinds of properties attract tenants?

The amount of rent you are asking is likely to be the single biggest factor of attracting a prospective tenant. There is nothing wrong with tenants wanting to pay less rent, and there is nothing wrong with you wanting to charge a higher rent. That's just business.

Properties with lower rents are likely to attract more prospective tenants than those that require a higher rent.

For this reason, the cost of the property is a factor. Not only the purchase price, but also the maintenance costs, will determine what rent is required. A property that can be acquired for a lower amount makes sense to most landlords. Properties that cost less to maintain are also desirable, because rent can be kept lower.

Everyone wants a nice place to live. Fresh paint, decent appliances, newer carpet, and bright lights can do a lot to improve the appearance and don't cost that much for the landlord to add to a rental unit. A clean unit also makes a great first impression. Often a good cleanup and freshening can do wonders to a rental property, making it much more attractive to a potential tenant.

#35. How do I determine competitive properties?

As a landlord, you should be watching for advertisements from others offering rentals. This is one of the best ways to determine what competitive properties are close to your rental. By watching these ads, it will not take long to determine what the going rate is for a unit such as yours.

Always try to compare your property to other similar units. Include factors such as location and basic features. Number of bedrooms, total rooms, baths, and features are important considerations. You should not compare a one-bedroom, one-bath apartment with a three-bedroom, two-bath house. There are too many nonmatching features.

The area you compare should be as close as possible to the neighborhood where your property is located. If possible, it should be in the same school district (many renters, especially those with children, often select a rental property based upon schools). The closer the comparison properties are to your property, the better your competitive analysis will be.

#36. **What is the best way to set the rent?**

Using your comparison analysis, you can quickly determine what the going rental rates are in your area. The more rental units you use for your comparisons, the more accurate your rent setting can be. In other words, it is better to compare six properties rather than two.

Don't use outdated comparisons to set the rent. Three months is about the maximum amount of time that you want to use for your rental rate information.

If you find that your rental comparisons indicate a range of $900 to $950 for similar units as yours, you have a good indication as to what your rate should be. When the ranges or spreads are much larger, it is harder to determine your asking rent. The best answer is to keep monitoring your competitive properties and get more comparisons.

Also keep in mind that you need to maintain a positive cash flow. For that reason, always consider what you must collect to remain profitable on your rental unit.

Your rent should always be set fairly, based on your local market. It should not be set solely on what your mortgage and expenses are.

#37. **Does it make sense to purchase a rental unit in a distant location?**

Most of the time, it does not. Being a distant landlord is almost always problematic. When you are not close by, little problems can become major ones. A leaky faucet that is not repaired could cause lots of damage because it was not repaired. Tenants could move out without notice, and your property could be vacant and vandalized without you knowing about it.

It is very difficult to manage and maintain your investment from a distant location. Living a short distance from your rental property always positions you in a better situation. Being able to get there quickly is a tremendous advantage.

Sometimes, you might be forced to become a distant landlord. This can happen due to an employment situation where you must move away. If you must relocate, ask a friend or relative to handle the rental management. Always offer some compensation for this service. Or, if that isn't possible, employ a professional management firm for your property.

#38.   Are vacation rentals good investments?

They can be, but they are different from renting units intended to be primary residences. Vacation rentals are usually short-term rentals, from a month, to a week, or even just a weekend. That means there is a constant turnover of the property from one tenant to the next. Some vacation rentals are by the season, which is often several months. The more the property is turned over, the more work is required by the landlord.

Paperwork in itself is increased by short-term rentals. You must process more rental agreements, collect and return security deposits, and handle reservation requests.

Another issue is cleaning the rental property after each rental has ended. Vacation properties are often used for parties. That in itself can be problematic. People will often break rules because it is impossible to evict a tenant legally during the short-term rental. Temporary renters often do not treat your property as well as they should. And you must often provide furnishings to make the property rentable to vacationers.

#39.   Should I rent a vacation property myself, or should I use a local rental agency?

If you are not nearby to handle the management, you should hire someone who is nearby. Depending on the location of your vacation rental property, it may be easy or difficult to find a management company. Major tourist locations have plenty of rental agencies. Properties located in rural or less popular vacation areas are harder to find a rental agency. Local real estate agents often provide this service for a fee. Some offer total service, including depositing funds directly into your bank account. Others provide only some services that you will need.

One of the things that you must be willing to do, if you are renting the property yourself, is market it. You need to maintain a constant marketing program to attract potential renters. Websites such as Vacation Renters by Owner *(www.vrbo.com)* are available to help the marketing process.

You must be well organized and be able to handle the additional paperwork. You must maintain a calendar for your reservations, and respond quickly to inquiries about your property. These are services a rental agency can do for you, or you can do yourself.

#40. Are there any types of vacation properties that I should avoid?

You should avoid vacation rental properties that are not easy to maintain. Properties requiring extensive repairs should also be passed on as potential vacation rental properties.

Units with single bedrooms are also best avoided. That's because you compete with Holiday Inn or Best Western. Units with two or more bedrooms often become more desirable and rentable.

Vacation properties are riskier investments than primary housing rental units. That's because vacation rentals are paid for with discretionary income. When there is a downturn in the economy, one of the things many Americans cut is vacations. They may continue to vacation, but renting a vacation property becomes less likely. To remain competitive, you may need to lower your rental fees.

Vacation rentals that offer amenities associated with leisure activities are also best. Hot tubs, pools, pool tables, media rooms or entertainment centers, decks, and other such amenities make the units more desirable. In addition, the proximity to such things as attractions, historic sites, golf courses, and restaurants also make a unit more desirable. You should avoid properties without these extras as rental investments.

#41. How many rental units should I acquire?

The best answer is probably as many as you possibly can! However, quantity is not as important as quality. You do not want any rental units that are not moneymaking opportunities.

Don't fall into the trap that it is always best to own many rental units. You should never attempt to own more than you can manage successfully and profitably. If properties cannot produce positive cash flow and profit for the landlord, there is no reason to buy it.

It makes sense to acquire additional rental units. Most successful landlords move from a single property to additional units. As they gain knowledge and experience, it becomes easier to manage more rental investment properties. But you can only accomplish so much in a day or a week. There gets to be a breaking point. Don't overdo it, and don't try to take on too much too quickly.

#42. What are the basic requirements of rental housing?

During the entire period of tenancy, the landlord must maintain the property in *habitable condition*. This definition may vary between localities, but it always means, at a minimum:

- Keep all common areas clean, accessible, and safe.
- Provide trash removal, and in most cases, trash and garbage containers.
- Maintain all mechanical systems, including electrical service, plumbing, sewage, heating or furnaces, and ventilation systems.
- Supply potable water, hot water, and heat.

- Provide a property with working locks, reasonable security, and safety equipment, such as working smoke detectors.
- Comply with all building codes.

Habitable condition is the basics any reasonable person should expect to provide when renting a property. No one can expect to rent (and continue to collect monthly rental payments) a property when they cannot deliver basic services, such as running, drinkable water, working plumbing, or electricity. It is only common sense that a landlord should provide things such as hot and cold water to a rental unit. To do less would mean the premises is not in a habitable condition.

#43. **What building codes must I know?**

Most building codes are extensive, encyclopedia-like books filled with technical specifications and complicated requirements. It is impractical for landlords to read, study, and know every single building code that might affect any rental unit. It makes far more sense to rely on professionals and their expertise to comply with codes.

Rely on licensed plumbers and electricians. Use professionals when you are making mechanical changes to your property. When you use professionals and they advise that a building code problem exists, fix it. Follow their recommendations to comply with your local codes.

Fixing building code errors can be costly and expensive. It can also become extremely costly to ignore the problem. At any time, the tenant could report the problem to the local municipality and a building inspector could be sent to visit your property.

Also, some code violations could become liability situations for the property owner. For example, a second floor balcony is made of wood, but over the years, the wood has rotted. The railings became loose, and the balcony is unsafe. If a tenant or a guest is injured from falling, the landlord is likely to be held responsible for this code violation.

#44.   **Are smoke detectors required in rental units?**

In most jurisdictions, smoke detectors are required in all rental units. Either state law or local ordinances require the installation of smoke detectors. For information on whether your community has adopted such ordinances, consult your local building, fire, or housing codes. Even if your property is in a location that does not require them, you should install them. They are inexpensive and extremely important.

Where they are required, at least one smoke detector must be installed by the landlord outside of each bedroom. If several bedrooms are served by the same hallway, one smoke detector may be installed in the corridor in the immediate vicinity of the bedrooms. In an efficiency apartment where the same room is used for dining, living, and sleeping purposes, the smoke detector must be located inside rather than outside the room. If there is a bedroom above the living or cooking area, a detector must be placed on the ceiling above the stairway.

Your local firefighters will certainly provide free advice and help on how and where to install smoke detectors. During your routine inspections of your property, make sure the smoke detectors are working by testing them.

#45.   **Am I required to have fire extinguishers in the rental property?**

Local or state laws may or may not require a fire extinguisher. You should supply one for each rental unit whether or not it is required.

Fire extinguishers are classified by the types of fires they can extinguish. There are three types of fires:

- Fires of ordinary products such as wood, cloth, and paper
- Fires that involve flammable liquids such as cooking grease, gasoline, kerosene, paint solvents, etc

■ Fires that involve electrical equipment

Fire extinguishers are labeled with the type of fire they will fight. ABC model fire extinguishers are the most popular type because they can be used for all three types of fires. Place the extinguisher in the kitchen.

You should inspect the fire extinguisher regularly to make sure it remains in working condition. Check the seal that secures the pin in the extinguisher handle. Check the extinguisher's gauge and feel the weight of the extinguisher to see if it is full.

#46. **What kind of locks must be on the doors?**

A landlord must provide locks. The rental unit must be able to be reasonably secured by the tenant. Some jurisdictions have established laws or regulations stating what the landlord must provide.

Generally, a landlord must install the following locks and security devices:

■ A window latch on each exterior window
■ A doorknob lock or keyed deadbolt on each exterior door
■ A sliding door pin lock on each exterior sliding glass door
■ A sliding door handle latch, or sliding door security bar on each exterior sliding glass door
■ A keyless bolting device (that only can be locked and unlocked from the inside) and a peephole on each exterior door

A landlord may not require a tenant to pay for repair or replacement of a lock if it breaks because of normal wear and tear. A landlord may require a tenant to pay for repair or replacement of a lock that was damaged by misuse of the tenant (or the tenant's family or guest).

#47. Are there other security safeguards that I must provide?

It depends on local laws. In some locales, landlords may be required to provide outside security lighting.

Fences may be necessary to provide security. They are usually installed around the perimeter of the property. These should be rod iron, as opposed to solid fences. This prevents criminals from hiding behind the fence. Fences also control access to and from the property. You may need to consider other alternatives that limit access to your rental property.

Security cameras are sometimes installed in corridors of apartment buildings. These cameras are hooked up to a DVD recorder, which records who enters or leaves the premises.

These additional security items are usually not required by local laws or ordinances. However, if your property has had a history of criminal activity, you may be found liable for not installing or upgrading security for the tenants and their guests. This is only likely to happen if someone is injured. They could claim negligence on your part and push for monetary damages.

#48. What appliances must I provide?

Few locales require landlords to furnish appliances such as refrigerators or stoves. Unless it is part of the lease agreement, the landlord is generally not required to supply appliances.

However, most do. From a practical standpoint, most landlords supply a stove and a refrigerator. Other common appliances include a dishwasher, clothes washer, and dryer. If you supply the appliance, you are responsible for its routine maintenance and for normal repairs.

One reason to supply these appliances is to make your rental unit more appealing to potential tenants. Including these appliances often entices the prospect to rent the property. Rent can be set higher, too, because of the extras being provided.

Another advantage of installing the appliances is that it eliminates tenants from moving appliances in and out of your unit. Large bulky items like appliances can damage your door jams or walls when being moved in and out of the premises.

Include your appliances in your lease agreement. A simple statement such as "the landlord will supply a stove and refrigerator" is all you need to prove later that the appliances are yours and not the tenants'.

#49. Must I provide communication connectivity, such as cable TV, telephone, or television antennas?

No. Unless there is a local ordinance or regulation, or a requirement in your lease agreement, you are not required to provide television, telephone, Internet, or other communication devices.

However, most landlords do provide access to cable television service and telephone service. The wiring inside the rental unit for these services is usually the landlord's responsibility, unless specified differently in the rental agreement.

Television antennas and satellite dishes are often restricted or prohibited. Most landlords do not want additional holes in their roof. There is also the issue of shoddy installation, which could cause damage or injuries during windstorms. To eliminate this possibility, many landlords do not permit the installation of any antenna or reception devices on their roofs.

Many tenants desire high-speed Internet access. This is often accomplished by telephone lines or TV cable.

#50. How should I handle the exterior maintenance of the property?

There are various methods successful landlords use to manage the exterior maintenance of their rental properties.

The most obvious option is to do the exterior maintenance yourself. Routine but varied visits to your property to perform the exterior maintenance are likely to keep tenants abiding by your rules. This allows you to keep a watchful eye on your investment. You can make sure trash and rubbish is being hauled away. Sweeping a sidewalk now and then demonstrates your desire to keep your property clean for your tenants.

Another option is to hire an exterior maintenance company. They will cut the grass, trim bushes, mulch, shovel snow, and do other exterior maintenance.

You could also require a tenant to do groundskeeping. This can be structured in any number of ways. You might give a reduced rent for the work or pay for the work separately. When using a tenant to do the exterior maintenance, it can become difficult if the tenant does not do the work you require. While it is easy to fire a company that doesn't show up to cut the grass every week, it is more difficult to fire a tenant that is not doing the work as agreed.

#51. **What should I do about common access areas?**

Multifamily properties have common areas. These are the areas where all the tenants have access on the property. Stairs, hallways, yards, sidewalks, laundries, and driveways are often common areas.

As the landlord, you are responsible to maintain all the common areas. This responsibilty cannot be passed off to a tenant. You must keep the area safe, clean, and in good repair. It could require daily or weekly maintenance, depending on the area and the amount of people accessing it.

The common area maintenance needs to be done by yourself or someone you hire. You can hire an individual (including a tenant) or a maintenance company. The maintenance responsibility and requirements can also be contractually assumed by a tenant, but a written agreement separate from the lease always makes sense. It's better to keep rent and maintenance payments separate, although many landlords do not do this. Many offer a reduced rent to a tenant to maintain the common access area. This can work, but it can become a problem should the tenant become slovenly with the maintenance work.

PART 2

Finding and Screening Tenants

FOR MOST LANDLORDS, the toughest part of renting a property is to find good tenants. Picking and choosing tenants often determines the success or failure of property rental. The tenant becomes the landlord's customer. This section of the book shows how to pick tenants, approve them, and do so without violating various laws that landlords must follow.

#52.   **What are the best ways to find tenants?**

Finding reliable tenants is a landlord's most important task. You need tenants that will pay the rent each month.

Sometimes a simple For Rent sign on the property is all it takes to generate inquires from potential tenants. Advertising the rental in the classified section of the local newspaper is another way to generate calls from people looking for a place to rent and live.

Today, listing the property for rent on the Internet is also a common practice. Websites such as craigslist *(www.craigslist.org)* offer renters a fast and convenient way to locate a rental unit. Many of the popular sites are free. Other sites include *www.rent.com, www.forrent.com,* and *www.move.com.*

Friends, coworkers, and relatives can also be a source of potential tenants. Receiving a referral from someone you know can often lead to finding a reliable tenant.

Another source of potential tenants is your real estate agent. Your agent often meets people that need a place to rent for a specific period because of a life-changing event, such as a divorce.

#53.   **Should I advertise for tenants?**

Yes. If you do not get a good amount of interest in the property from a sign, then there is nothing wrong with advertising for prospective tenants. Many people, when looking for a place to rent, will look in the local newspaper for ads offering rentals.

Your advertisement cannot violate the Fair Housing laws. Landlords get in trouble when they focus on the tenant they are seeking rather than a property.

An acceptable advertisement looks like this:

Quaker Hills — 3 BR, 1½ BA with large yard, fireplace, central a/c. $1,050 per month, utilities included. Kitchen recently renovated. New carpet throughout. Available December 1.

An unacceptable advertisement looks like this:

Wilshire Hills — 2 BR, 1 BA apartment. No children. Bachelors preferred. $750 month. Available January 1.

Most newspaper publishers will assist you in writing an ad that is not discriminatory. However, if you post an ad online, you are not permitted to violate the Fair Housing laws. Landlords have been successfully prosecuted for online advertising violations.

#54. Should I use a real estate agent to find tenants?

Real estate agents can often locate a tenant for you. People that do not have enough money for a down payment or are in a life-changing event need rental housing. As part of their regular work, agents are in constant contact with people seeking housing.

When working with an agent, you can expect either a simple referral (where you do all the work, from showing the property, screening the prospective tenant, executing a lease), or the agent doing all this work for you. When the agent is doing this work, it is common for a fee of one month's rent to be paid by the landlord to the agent. The amount of the agent's fee is negotiable.

If you have a working relationship with an agent, you are more likely to get a referral from the agent. A quick phone call or e-mail from you can alert the agent of your unit's availability. You are likely to get more activity if you are willing to pay the agent for finding a tenant for you. Decide ahead of time as to what you want from the agent, and be prepared to discuss this with the agent before they begin work. An agent may be willing to help you find a tenant if it involves little work, and if the agent believes you will be coming back when you want to buy or sell a property.

#55. **Is it safer to rent to a friend or relative than a stranger?**

You should never rent one of your units to anyone that you cannot or will not evict. Your unit is part of your rental business. Whether you own one or a hundred units, every tenancy should be considered a business decision.

When you rent a unit to a relative or a friend, you are crossing the line of this rental remaining a mere business transaction. Adding the element of a friendship or family to the transaction changes the dynamic of the business transaction. It becomes complicated and can become unmanageable.

Renting a unit to your mom is a nice thing to do, but when you do, you have lost the business aspect of the transaction. You can't evict your mom. It's that simple. When you rent to a relative, you are renting to someone you are connected to for the rest of your life.

Friends are a bit different. If things go sour, you might end up losing your friendship over the rental. Before you ever consider renting to a friend or a relative, ask yourself if you could evict that person without any reservations.

#56. **What is the correct way to show a property to a prospective tenant?**

After making an appointment with a prospective tenant, you and the tenant meet at the rental property for a showing. This allows the prospective tenant to look at the property. It is best for the tenant to be allowed to walk through the property. Point out the features of the property—such as storage areas, appliances, and other amenities. Be prepared to answer general questions about the property, such as heating or cable service.

Don't say anything that could be construed as steering or suggesting one unit over another, based on the applicant. Allow the applicant to decide about renting the unit without suggestions about how it could (or could not) be used based on the possible occupants.

An occupied rental unit often causes challenges for the landlord. To show the property when occupied by a current tenant requires that you first give notice to the tenant—usually twenty-four hours in advance. Your notice should be in writing, but it can also be by telephone. Tenants may not have the property in the best condition for a showing. Depending on the tenant, a sloppy or slovenly appearance can be everywhere, from dirty towels in the bathroom or laundry on the floor, to a kitchen sink full of dirty dishes. There is little, if anything, you can do about this.

#57. How can I legally screen a tenant?

Screening a tenant may seem perilous, but it is not that difficult. You must first set up rules that do not discriminate based on race, religion, marital status, etc. Once you know the rules, you can then move toward screening a tenant.

A good example of this might be that you would establish a rule that no pets are permitted in your rental unit. You would then be permitted to ask if the proposed tenant has a pet. If the tenant has a pet, you would reject their application for tenancy, and decline to rent the property to them. It would be an automatic rejection, based on your rule, and not based on who the tenant is.

Don't fear the screening process. As a landlord, you must follow the law, but you do not have to rent to everyone or anyone that might apply.

Remember to treat all applicants the same. You should not ask one applicant to complete an application, and another not to do so. You are best to have rental rules established, in writing, and give a copy to all applicants. It is one way to prove you are treating all potential tenants equally and fairly.

#58. What should I ask a prospective tenant?

To prevent any misunderstanding, you should provide an application to anyone seeking tenancy. The application should request:

- The prospective tenant(s)' full name, address, phone number, and social security number
- The length of time the applicant has lived at the current address
- The name and phone number of the current and past landlords
- The name, address, and phone number of the current employer
- The applicant's current income
- Credit references
- Personal references

You might also ask other information to determine if your proposed tenant can and will comply with your established rules. If your rules prohibit waterbeds, you might ask if the tenant owns or plans to purchase one for use in your rental unit.

To verify identity, you should also request some form of government issued identification, such as a driver's license, passport, or green card. Photo identification is always best. A copy of the last pay stub allows quick verification of employment and income.

You should also request an authorization to release information to you. This authorization, when signed by the applicant, will allow credit references and employers to release information to you. It is common for many references and employers not to release any information to you without a copy of the release in their records. Employers may not verify an applicant's employment without first receiving a copy of the release. Most credit references and employers that require the release will accept it via fax.

#59. What kind of application form should I use?

Your application form should be a printed, standard form approved for use in your jurisdiction. Don't fall into the trap of preparing your own application or downloading a form from the Internet.

Rather, acquire an application from your local real estate attorney. Most applications are usually one or two pages.

Any supplemental questions, such as possessions, pets, or habits (like smoking), should be prepared by your attorney and made a part of the application process.

Many landlords stumble during the application process. Although well-meaning, what might seem like a legitimate question could be determined later to have been discriminatory or even illegal. Avoid any legal jeopardy by getting help first from your lawyer. By getting the forms from your attorney and asking the proposed tenant to complete them, you can be sure that you are not violating the law.

Be sure to provide an application to anyone that asks for one. Also, do not hesitate to provide copies of your tenancy rules and qualifications. It is best to have your attorney review your rules to make sure they are proper and comply with the current law.

#60.   Who should complete the application?

All prospective adult tenants should complete the application for tenancy. The parties that sign the application should be the same that will be on the lease agreement, if you decide to lease your unit to the applicants.

You want as much information as possible about your applicants. Hopefully, you will be able to file this information away into a folder and never need to refer to it again. But when things go sour, you will want the information from the application.

If you rent a unit to a single person (an unmarried individual) be sure to ask whom to contact in case of an emergency. It might be a parent, child, or sibling, but you do need to know whom you should contact when something goes wrong (for example, the tenant falls down and is taken unconscious to the hospital). Information from the application is how you would know whom to contact.

#61. **May I charge an application fee?**

Unless there is a local regulation prohibiting the fee, landlords can generally charge an application fee. The potential tenant pays an application fee to a rental property owner, in order that the owner can screen the background of the potential tenant before signing the lease. Application fees for rental properties should not exceed the cost of the screening process, which may include criminal background checks, credit history, and rental history of the prospective tenant. Criminal background checks can be completed via the Internet.

If your established screening procedures incur fees of $25, then you should charge $25 for the application fee. Standard and prudent fees would be what you must pay for a credit check, criminal history check, or other similar records checks. Don't try to make money on the application fees. The idea is to cover your costs.

In locales where application fees are regulated, you will likely be required to provide a copy of your tenancy approval policy. Some locales may require you to refund or credit the application fee if tenancy is offered and accepted by the applicant. Most will also require landlords to provide a receipt for any application fee collected.

#62. **Can I restrict prospective tenants from having specific possessions, such as motorcycles or waterbeds?**

Yes, you can restrict your tenants from storing or using possessions that are likely to cause damage or harm to your property, prevent others from the peaceful enjoyment of their property, or are, by their very nature, illegal or harmful.

A tenant who kept a collection of poisonous snakes or stored gunpowder in the rental unit could be evicted because of this activity. As a landlord, you would only need to convince a judge of the danger. No judge is going to condone this type of activity, so you do not need a rulebook of every possible dangerous activity or possession.

However, for other items, it may not be so clear. Your best defense is to establish the ground rules before your tenant takes possession of the rental unit, and then be vigilant in enforcing your rules. An example might be that waterbeds are not permitted because of the damage they might cause to your rental unit. Establish a rule that waterbeds are prohibited on the property. If your tenant then sets up a waterbed, it is clear grounds for eviction. By having this rule established, in writing, it will be easier to convince a judge that your tenant deserves eviction and to rule in your favor.

#63. Is a first come, first served policy legal and effective?

Not only is a first come, first served policy legal, it is probably your best defense in showing that you are not being discriminatory in your tenancy selection policy. By establishing this policy, you can offer tenancy to the first applicant that qualifies by meeting your selection criteria.

It is probably safe for you to announce your first come, first served policy on your tenancy qualification and selection criteria by stating that the first applicant who applies and is approved will be offered a lease for the rental unit.

When you establish this policy, make sure your potential tenants understand that others may apply while you are processing their application. Advise all tenant applicants that any delay could result in someone else getting an application completed first. For that reason, they should not hesitate in providing the information needed to process the application. All prospective tenants should understand clearly that not providing information requested or needed might result in the rejection of their application.

#64. What selection criteria should I follow?

The selection process should be procedural and unemotional. Before the selection process commences, the tenant should either qualify or not.

For example, you might decide that a tenant's monthly income must be four times the monthly rent. If your unit rents for $900, the prospective tenant's gross monthly income must be $3,600. If the tenant cannot prove or you cannot verify a minimum of $3,600, then the tenant's application should be rejected. If the tenant's monthly income is $3,600 or more, then move on to the next part of the selection criteria.

Your selection criteria should be based upon the tenant's willingness and ability to pay the monthly rent and to take possession of the property as a residence without damaging it.

The past provides a good judgment of future performance. That's the reason credit reports become important. By looking at a prospective tenant's credit report, you can tell how likely it is that the tenant will pay the rent. An applicant's past credit report that is filled with evictions, landlord disputes, and rent judgments indicates applicant is not likely to pay rent on time. An applicant with few credit issues is more likely to be a good tenant, and one that will not deliberately damage the rental unit.

#65. How can I verify employment?

Verifying employment is not a difficult process. You can often quickly verify employment and income from most employers via the telephone.

Some employers have a loose verification process, while others have a strict procedure in place. Some will require written authorization, while others will simply verify that a person is employed, how long they have been employed, their job title, and confirm the pay rate. They will not tell you everything, but if you ask if Suzy Smith is employed there as an assembler, they will say yes or no. This is routine, and is usually done by someone in the personnel or human resources division.

Some landlords accept the last paycheck as the employment verification. But it is always best to call the prospective tenant's employer and verify what the tenant has told you. By doing so, you are confirming what has been told to you, and you are sending a strong message that you are operating a legitimate business. You are signaling to your future tenant that you will handle all business appropriately.

#66. **During the screening process, what should I be looking for?**

There are three main areas that you should be considering when deciding to accept a tenant. They include:

- The willingness and the ability to make the rental payment to you each month
- A reasonable expectation that your tenant will not use your property for any illegal activity
- The willingness and the ability to abide by the rental lease agreement and rental rules you ask the potential tenant to sign before taking possession of your rental unit

Prospective tenants that do not have employment or provable income from regular sources (such as pension funds or investments), but do have large sums of cash, should be suspect. Applicants that have a long or colorful history of evictions are questionable about their ability to live within the terms of a lease agreement. Tenants without the ability (income) to make the monthly rent payment should also be rejected.

#67. **How much time do I have to screen an applicant?**

There may or may not be local laws that set the amount of time you have to approve or reject a tenant. You should move quickly with any application, and make your decision within two to three days.

To move quickly with a tenant's application, you must use the telephone effectively. You will need to check references, employment, and verify other information. Doing so by mail is time consuming.

If you take too long to approve or reject a tenant's application, the tenant will likely move on to another rental unit. This might mean you lost a good tenant that would have been your customer over the next year or more. Delaying the approval or rejection might also be construed as a method you are using to discriminate against prospective tenants.

It is always best to process the application as promptly as possible. It is to your benefit to approve an applicant and get a lease signed as soon as you can. Obviously, getting the unit rented is your ultimate goal. Responding quickly to a potential tenant is a good way to turn them into a customer for your rental property business.

#68. Can I use a minimum income requirement to screen tenants?

Yes, you can use a minimum income requirement, as long as you do so with all prospective tenants. To show that you are not picking and choosing prospective tenants for any reason other than their income level, you should put your policy in writing.

You might develop a policy where the tenant must have three times the amount of the rent for a monthly income. For example, if your rent is $1,000 per month, the prospective tenant must have a gross monthly income of $3,000 or more. If the tenant can prove this income from legitimate sources (employment, court-ordered child support, pension, social security, etc.), then the tenant is qualified to rent your property. It is either a yes or no—either they have the cash flow each month to pay the rent, or they don't. If they can't prove that they have the income, then reject their application in writing.

By putting the monthly income requirement in writing, you show your policy. Stick to whatever you decide for a minimum income. Don't deviate from applicant to applicant.

#69.   **What is the best way to verify a prospective tenant's income?**

You can telephone the applicant's employer and ask to verify employment and income. Most employers will verify. In other words, if you supply the information, the employer will agree (or disagree) with what you say the applicant has supplied.

Some employers will do so without a written authorization. Others will require a written release signed by their employee before speaking with you. They will often accept a fax of the signed authorization in order to speed up the verification process.

A fast way is to ask for the last two paycheck stubs of the applicant. The current weekly pay is easily determined from the stubs. But go a bit further by looking at the year to date income. With the use of a calculator, you can quickly determine what the tenant's monthly income is. The pay stubs will quickly allow you to determine if the applicant's income is sufficient to qualify.

Use the same type of official documentation to verify other sources of income. For example, if an applicant is using court-ordered child support as part of the income needed to qualify for the rental unit, ask for proof of that income in the form of the court order, check stubs, or electronic fund transfers to the prospect's bank accounts.

#70.   **How can I check a prospective tenant's credit?**

There are three major credit bureaus. They are:

Equifax
P.O. Box 740256
Atlanta, GA 30374
(800) 685-1111
www.equifax.com

Experian
P.O. Box 2002
Allen, TX 75013
(888) 397-3742
www.experian.com

TransUnion LLC
P.O. Box 2000
Chester, PA 19022
(800) 888-4213
www.transunion.com

You can purchase a credit report from sources online or from your local credit bureau. Your local bureau often has a business relationship with one of the three bureaus. The cost for the credit report varies, but it is usually between $15 to $25. There are different types of credit reports available. Some are more extensive than others, and cost more.

Some local landlord associations often have arranged for its members to obtain credit reports of prospective tenants. Don't accept any credit report supplied by a prospective tenant. It is easy for anyone with a computer and some basic software to create, forge, or modify documents.

#71. May I charge a fee for a credit check?

Generally, you can charge a fee for a credit report. Some local municipalities may have established rules as to the maximum amount you can collect. It is best not to look at the cost of getting a credit report as a profit center for your business. You should simply collect from the tenant what you must pay for the report—nothing more or less (unless you are limited by local regulations as to what you can collect, and that amount is less than your cost).

Be clear with your application instructions that a check for a specific amount is required for a credit report. If you are going to obtain credit reports, get one for each applicant for all your rental units. Be sure to get a credit report for each prospective tenant. If your application shows a proposed joint tenancy (two or more people), get a credit report for each person. Collect a fee for each credit report you request from the credit bureau.

#72. What should I look for on a credit report?

The first thing to check is to make sure the credit report matches your proposed tenant. Be sure that everything makes sense. For example, if your proposed tenant is a mid-twenties female that has lived in your town for the past ten years, but the report shows the subject is thirty years older and has lived in five different states in the past two years, something is not correct. You will be surprised how many credit reports have erroneous information, or how many reports you might order that will be delivered on a different person. Don't expect to see perfect credit. You are looking for trends, such as repeated late payments or writeoffs. Of course, you are also looking for judgments from other landlords or uncollected rent that is still owed.

Consumer credit accounts that are generally paid on time indicate willingness to pay as agreed and the ability to live within one's means.

#73. Should I rent to someone with perfect rental history but poor consumer credit?

The credit decision is always up to you. Some people have poor consumer credit but always pay their rent on time. You may be surprised to get a "perfect" credit report from a former or current landlord, yet the consumer credit is terrible. That's just the way some people live.

One landlord had a tenant for twenty-three years, and during that entire time, the tenant only missed the rent payment once: when she was injured at work, she called the landlord to say she would be late with the rent until she received her disability check. It was thirteen days late, but she made the rent payment.

When the landlord decided to sell the property, it was offered first to the tenant. Although her payment record was well established, the tenant's consumer credit report was horrendous. No one would finance her purchase of the property. The landlord eventually sold the property to this tenant by carrying the financing on the property.

#74. Should I ask for references?

You should always ask a prospective renter for references. As part of your rental process, routinely ask for references on your application. It is also helpful to ask for emergency contacts at the same time ("in case of an emergency, whom should we call?").

Having this information in your file might become very useful. Having a relative or close friend's name can be used to track down someone who might skip out on you.

Always include a statement above the signature line on your application that grants you permission to contact employers and landlords and to pull criminal and credit checks, both during the application process and in the future.

Don't just ask for references. Call them. Tell the person you are calling that their name was given as a reference. Record the responses. Ask generic questions like, "Can you give a positive reference?" or "Is there any reason why the premises should not be rented to this person?"

Listen carefully for hesitation on the part of the person you called. They know your tenant much better than you do. Be alert for any negative remarks or comments.

#75.   **What am I allowed to ask a reference about a prospective tenant?**

Generally, you should ask a reference the same questions you would ask the prospective tenant. Your inquiry should be one that confirms the good character of your applicant.

Ask how long the reference has known the prospective tenant. It is better to get the reference to talk or chat with you. For some, this is easier if you first prepare a form with the questions you want to ask. Then it is just a matter of reading the questions from this form.

Ask the reference to confirm facts the applicant has supplied to you. For example, ask the reference, "Can you confirm that the applicant has lived at 123 Washington Street for the last four years?"

You can ask the reference to confirm the size of your applicant's family.

Ask generic questions that tend to get the reference to talk or chat with you. Avoid questions that tend to have a yes or no answer. Ask questions that require longer responses, such as, "How would you describe the applicant's work history?" rather than, "Does the applicant have a good work history?"

#76.   **What questions am I allowed to ask a tenant?**

As part of the application and approval process, you will have routine questions that you need to ask. The information landlords want in order to screen applicants generally falls into these categories:

- Income and employment
- Rental history
- Eviction history
- Credit history

Basic information, such as name, current address, employment, and past addresses, are routine. The prospective tenant expects questions designed to solicit this general information.

You can also ask questions and seek information that allows you to identify the applicant. This includes prospective tenant's Social Security Number, driver's license number, and date of birth. You should use this information to make certain any information you check about the tenant is accurate. You should always photocopy a government-issued identification document that verifies identity, such as a driver's license or passport.

Questions designed to make certain the applicant can and will comply with your established rules are generally allowed. For example, you may have established a "no pets" rule for the property. As part of the application process, you can ask if the tenant has any pets.

All adults that will be living in your premises should be asked to complete an application.

#77. **What questions am I not allowed to ask a tenant?**

There are probably hundreds of questions that you cannot legally ask a tenant as part of the screening process. The general rules are that you cannot ask questions that allow you to discriminate against any applicant.

According to HUD (U.S. Department of Housing and Urban Development), the rental of housing is clearly controlled. HUD says that no one may take any of the following actions based on race, color, national origin, religion, sex, familial status, or handicap:

- Refuse to rent or sell housing
- Refuse to negotiate for housing
- Make housing unavailable
- Deny a dwelling

- Set different terms, conditions, or privileges for rental of a dwelling
- Provide different housing services or facilities
- Falsely deny that housing is available for inspection or rental

In other areas, there are additional regulations that also prohibit discrimination based on occupation, sexual orientation, or immigration status.

Questions designed to discriminate are not permitted. However, the laws do not mean you cannot turn down an applicant. An applicant that has too little income or a record of bad debt can be denied.

#78.   What is steering?

The funneling of renters to a particular unit is called steering. It is illegal and a violation of the Fair Housing laws. Often a violation can be intentional, or it could happen through an innocent act. For example, suppose you have a two-unit building, and both units are available. A prospective tenant who happens to be wheelchair bound comes to see the property. You naturally only show the lower unit, logically thinking the upper unit would not be suitable. You have just steered the potential renter, most probably by trying to be helpful.

Steering is when the landlord decides which unit an applicant can have instead of allowing the tenants to choose for themselves. Steering can only occur when the tenant is in a protected class. According to the U.S. Housing and Urban Development (HUD), housing discrimination cannot be based on race, color, national origin, religion, sex, family status, or disability. People in these categories are the protected class. Some states have expanded the protected classes; for example, prohibiting discrimination on the basis of age or sexual orientation.

You could establish a policy of not allowing dog owners in upper apartments, because you are trying to minimize noise. Pet owners are not a protected class. Establishing a policy of keeping families with small children out of the upper apartment would be a Fair Housing violation because they are a protected class.

#79. Does HUD really enforce the Fair Housing and Equal Housing Opportunity Laws on small-business landlords?

Absolutely. Violations of these laws are serious offenses. HUD dedicates resources to maintain the strict compliance with all sections of the laws. It does not matter if the landlord is large or small. HUD strives to enforce the housing laws uniformly.

Each month, HUD posts new cases of violations on the HUD website. Many of the housing law violations may have happened years ago, but that does not curtail the enforcement actions. If a violation occurred months or years before, HUD will still investigate and seek court action against the landlord.

Don't think that the cases are only about discrimination based on sex or race. Other areas of potential Fair Housing violations include offering senior citizen discounts or attempting to limit the number of children in a rental unit. You can, for example, limit the number of occupants in your units, but you may not limit the number of children. Two occupants per bedroom is a good and prudent standard for occupancy limitations. Therefore, a two-bedroom apartment could accommodate a single parent and three children. It would be a violation of the Fair Housing law to establish a policy of only two children per unit. However, you can establish a policy of no more than two occupants per bedroom.

#80. Should I contact current or past landlords?

Yes. As part of the screening process, always contact the current and past landlords of the applicant(s). Don't overlook this important process.

Before contacting the previous or current landlords, always obtain written permission from your prospective tenants.

If an applicant provides you with copies of cancelled rent payment checks, accept them, but always check with the current landlord. The applicant might be in a heated dispute with the current landlord and is now providing you with the check copies in an attempt to prevent your contact. Remember that tenants are not evicted solely for nonpayment of rent. They are just as often evicted for rules violations or damaging property.

Look for any gaps in rental history. If there is a gap of several months, determine why. It could be another sign of your prospective tenant trying to cover a past problem by not telling you of an address where he or she lived.

Unless a local regulation prohibits it, look at the past three years of rental history.

#81.   **What can I ask a current or past landlord about the prospective tenant?**

You can ask the previous and past landlords questions that verify the applicant's information and how he or she was as a tenant. Don't forget to ask if the landlord would rent (or would continue to rent) to the applicant again.

Ask if during the tenancy whether the applicant complied with all the terms of the lease and followed the rules. Of course, you would ask if the rent was paid on time and as agreed.

Don't forget to ask the current landlord to verify the address of the property the tenants are leaving from. You may be surprised how many phony reference "landlords" don't even know their friend's address or how long the tenancy was. Don't put it past bad applicants to have a friend or relative pose as a landlord, especially when they think you will be checking.

Ask targeted questions, and always confirm information given. For example, confirm that date of rental.

Your purpose is to determine if the applicant is likely to pay the rent and live in your property under the terms of the lease. By checking with past landlords, you can determine how likely the tenant will live peacefully and problem-free in your property.

#82.   **What is a tenant screening service?**

There are all types of tenant screening services available to landlords. Most provide landlords access to a credit reporting service inexpensively (and without the necessity and expense of joining a credit bureau).

Many of these tenant screening services are available on the Internet, such as *www.tenantscreening.com* or *www.e-renter.com* (typing "tenant screening service" into any search engine will generate many services). These companies search databases of judgments and court documents, as well as credit reports, and then generate a report for you. Depending on how in depth of a report you want, the cost can vary from $15–$20, and go as high as $150–$200.

Many tenant screening services also perform criminal background checks. Many provide nationwide criminal and credit checks, and statewide judgment checks.

Most of the services provide nearly instant results. Because of the speed of the Internet and the computers, databases are quickly accessed and you can have a result of your inquiry in minutes, if not seconds.

Don't use any tenant screening service unless you have first obtained written authorization from the applicant.

#83. **Am I allowed to ask for identification from a prospective tenant?**

Yes, as a landlord, you are permitted to ask for identification from a tenant. You should do so for each applicant seeking to lease your premises.

Only accept government issued photo identification documents. A photo identification issued by a local college, school, or business may be presented, but also seek a government issued ID. Don't settle for less.

With today's rampant identity theft problems, make sure you are given the original document. Do not accept photocopies of any identification in lieu of seeing the actual document. Photocopies may be convenient, but they are not prudent. Look at the identification, and make sure the person on the document is the person sitting across from you.

Accept no excuses. If an adult cannot produce the required identification, deny the application. Make it a hard and fast rule that government issued identification is required to rent your property.

#84. **How do I reject an applicant?**

Always reject an applicant in writing. Never reject verbally without a written follow-up.

Once a landlord takes an adverse action, the Fair Credit Reporting Act (FCRA) requires the landlord to send a notice to the applicant informing the prospective tenant of the action taken and advising him or her of rights under the FCRA, including the right to obtain a consumer report from the screening service or credit bureau, to dispute inaccurate information, or to request further information from the landlord when the adverse action is based on information other than the consumer report.

If you are rejecting because of information received from a credit report or screening service, you must notify the applicant of the entity that provided the information. Your notice should also include contact information. Always keep a copy of your notification.

If your reason for a denial is other than one based on credit history, write a letter, and explain briefly the basis for the rejection. For example, if the applicant does not qualify because of insufficient income, simply state that reason. (See Appendix A for a sample letter.)

#85. How do I accept an applicant?

Always accept an applicant in writing.

It is certainly acceptable to notify the applicant by telephone, but always follow up a telephone call with written communication. Your letter should be mailed promptly. It is likely that your prospective tenant may be looking at other potential living arrangements. Now that you decided the applicant would make a good tenant, you do not want to lose the tenant.

Your letter should confirm that you have approved their application, and you should include all the basic terms and conditions of the rental.

The correspondence should include the length of the rental, the starting date of the occupancy, the amount of the monthly rent, security deposit, and other pertinent information.

It is not necessary to cover all the terms and conditions of the lease in this acceptance correspondence. However, you should also state how much money is due and required to accept the occupancy of your unit. (See Appendix A for a sample letter.)

#86. How long should approved applicants have to accept my offer of renting the property to them?

All offers of rental to an approved applicant should include a deadline to accept the terms and conditions you are offering. Don't extend any offer without a date of acceptance. The amount of time should be minimal.

You do not want to be in limbo waiting for the applicant to decide to accept your rental. You may want to limit the amount of time for acceptance to five or seven days, or give a specific date. The reason is simple: if the new tenant does not accept your offer, you want to continue your search for the next applicant.

Many successful landlords use the telephone to notify the new tenant of the approval. This stops the tenant from applying and looking elsewhere.

Some landlords will allow the tenant to pay the security deposit, and then wait until the end of the month to collect the first month's rent. After that is paid, the tenant is then given the keys and the possession of the property.

#87.   **Do I need to use a written lease?**

Yes. Never rent your unit without a written and signed lease. This advice is just as important if the renter is a relative, friend, or stranger.

Your lease grants legal rights (such as occupancy, possession, use) of the premises to the tenant. The tenant agrees to specific terms and conditions, as you do as the landlord. Without a formal written lease, many legal issues become cloudy, at best.

There are many "standard" lease forms available from various sources. The best advice for any landlord is to obtain a lease form from a local attorney. Terms, conditions, and phrases vary among the states. The lease is designed to protect your property. Make sure all provisions are enforceable in court by getting the lease from your lawyer.

Your attorney will advise you if the lease needs to be notarized. In some jurisdictions, this is a requirement. When something goes bad—and no matter how careful you are, something will go bad eventually—you need to have the lease to show to a small claims judge.

#88. **What should be included in a lease?**

Each lease is different. They vary from state to state, and can even vary from counties within each state. There is no such thing as a universal lease agreement that is workable for all jurisdictions.

The lease is a contract, and as such, it must contain many basic, identifying factors. The lease, as far as a landlord is concerned, should be a fill-in-the-blanks form. In addition to filling in your own name and address, you are also filling in the name(s) and address(es) of the tenants. The property to be rented, the amount of rent, the way it is to be paid, the length of the occupancy, and other similar factors are included in all leases.

Leases commonly describe the requirements of both parties. It is here where the landlord and the tenant agree who pays other expenses, such as electricity or gas.

How the lease terminates if the property becomes uninhabitable (such as a fire) is described. When the tenants do not pay rent, the handling of the security deposit and other similar items are part of standard lease agreements.

#89. **Should I rent a property for a one-year period?**

Yes. For residential units, the common rental period is twelve months (one year). There are times when you might want to make the lease for a different period. For example, your tenant may be attending college or a university from September to May. You may want to lease the property for those months.

It seldom becomes an issue to rent a property for more or less time than the standard twelve months. Turnover of the rental unit is expensive and time consuming for the landlord. Keeping a tenant in the property for the next year is always a reassuring thought to most successful landlords.

Seasonal properties (especially vacation rentals) are often rented for less than twelve months.

Six or nine-month leases are also common. Many leases convert to a month-to-month lease after the initial period.

Unless there is some reason why you would not want to sign a lease for less or more than twelve months, it makes good business sense to do so. By being flexible with the length of your leasing term, you may be able to charge more for the monthly rent and attract a worthy tenant.

#90. **When does a month-to-month rental make sense?**

There are many occasions when a month-to-month lease or rental agreement makes sense. With a month-to-month lease, either the tenant or the landlord can notify the other party that they want to terminate the lease within the next thirty days. They simply move their possessions within the month, and the rental unit is vacated.

Some tenants are simply more comfortable with a month-to-month lease. It gives them a greater feeling of security to know they can move, should they have any reason to do so. A landlord prefers the longer lease term (especially those that have a monthly mortgage payment on the property). Renters that may be transferred because of job relocation or extensive travel often prefer the month-to-month lease.

Some successful landlords use the month-to-month lease as a tool to identify problem tenants. Rather than be "stuck" with a difficult tenant for an extended period, the thirty-day lease allows the landlord to terminate the rental and get the tenant out within a month.

#91. **Where can I get a blank lease to use?**

There are many sources for blank lease forms. Most real estate agents have ready access to the forms, in electronic format or printed paper.

Many will give the forms to a landlord in the hope of developing a working business relationship.

Another source of rental agreements is local investor groups that meet for the purpose to discuss common problems, learn about being a landlord, and to hear guest speakers. It may take a little bit of work to locate such a group, but they do exist in most locations throughout the country.

Stationery stores also sell lease agreements. Title or abstract companies generally have ready access to blank rental forms. Many different software programs generate "ready-to-sign" leases or rental agreements. The Internet is full of examples and sample lease agreements.

Unless the blank lease form is obtained from your attorney, you should ask your lawyer to review and approve the lease agreement you intend to use.

#92. Should I require that my tenant purchase tenants' insurance?

Yes, you should require that all tenants have renters' or tenants' insurance. It is relatively inexpensive, and it protects the tenant's property against loss due to fire, theft, vandalism, and other unintended causes.

When a tenant suffers a loss, they are far less likely to attempt to blame you for the loss if they can recover from an insurance policy. For example, if property is stolen, the tenant may decide to claim that as the landlord, you did not provide adequate locks or security. However, if their loss is mitigated because of an insurance payment, there is a far less likely chance that you will ever be presented with any claim.

Renters' insurance also covers claims of negligence. When a tenant's actions cause injury or property damage to another, the renters' insurance protects against the liability lawsuit. An example is when a guest slips and falls on a wet kitchen floor, breaking an arm. The renters' insurance protects the tenant against any injury claim.

The strategy is simple: because the tenant is covered by insurance for losses, the tenant will not be looking to you for reimbursement.

#93. What is the difference between a Certificate of Insurance and an Additional Named Insured document from a property insurer?

There is a big difference. When purchasing insurance, the policy owner (sometimes called the policy holder) is the named insured. This distinction is important: the named insured has all the benefits of the insurance.

Insurers issue two types of documents that benefit other than the named insured. They are:

1. Certificate of Insurance
2. Additional Named Insured

The Certificate of Insurance does not afford any insurance protection to a person that receives the certificate. It simply states that insurance is in place, according to the terms and conditions of the policy.

The Additional Named Insured affords insurance protection. All the benefits of the policy are afforded to the person on the Additional Named Insured form, but that person does not pay the insurance premium.

It is best to be an additional named insured on the renter's insurance policy. Should a liability claim or lawsuit be filed against you and the tenant, the renter's insurance policy provides protection to you.

#94. **When do I collect the security deposit?**

The security deposit is generally collected at the time the lease is signed. The amount of the security deposit was established with the earlier contact with the tenant.

It is often best to ask for two separate payments. Request a check for the security deposit, and another check for the rent.

Make sure the security deposit check is clearly identified as the payment for the security deposit. Make a photocopy of the check, and retain it in your tenant file. You want to make sure that you can clearly show the amount of the security deposit. If you combine the security payment with a rent payment, it becomes unclear.

Make sure the intent of the security deposit is clear. It should be your desire to return 100 percent of the security deposit to the tenant at the end of the rental. As long as the property is not damaged, you will do so. If there is damage, you will repair that damage and pay for the repairs from the security deposit.

#95. **What is the maximum amount of security deposit I can impose?**

The standard security deposit is equivalent to one month's rent. However, unless restricted by law, you can set the security deposit at any amount that you want. You could rent your property without a security deposit or with an exceptionally high security deposit.

The higher the security deposit, however, the more difficult it will be to find a tenant. Good tenants won't necessarily have lots of extra cash to turn over to you to hold as a security deposit. They will simply find another rental unit.

If you allow pets, it is common to ask for an additional security deposit. A dog or cat can cause extensive damage. At the minimum, when the tenant leaves the premises, you are likely going to need to have all carpets professionally cleaned.

On a bad day, a pet can destroy a carpet. Collecting an extra $50 or so as a security deposit when a pet is in the property could be inadequate to pay for damage. And no pet owner will ever tell a landlord that the pet would cause damage.

#96. **Are there any special restrictions on how I handle the tenant's security deposit?**

The security deposit is not income. You should always consider the security deposit as money that you will need to pay back either to the tenant or to a repairperson. For that reason, the security deposit should be placed in an interest-bearing account.

Keep the security deposits you collect separated from your other funds. Always be prepared to return the deposit.

Landlords and tenants often get into disputes over security deposits. It is often the most contentious issue over the rental. Should you not return the security deposit on time, the tenant is usually, by law, given the right to collect additional damages from you. The amount can be double or triple the amount of the security deposit. You do not want to be in the position of not being able to return a security deposit because you do not have the funds. This is why you should never co-mingle security deposits with your regular operating money. Keep the security deposits separate, and never look at it as your money.

#97. **What creative methods can I use to market my property?**

Many landlords allow their rental units to remain empty by not properly marketing them. A few extra words in a classified advertisement can make the difference of the phone ringing or not. For example, adding descriptive words like "bright" or "cheery" can excite a potential tenant.

Sell your unit with emotion. "Enjoy your morning coffee on the private porch" is much better than simply writing "porch" in an advertisement.

Use the Internet to attract tenants. Websites like craigslist or Kijiji offer free or inexpensive ads for most areas. Add photographs to show your property to those browsing the Internet for a rental unit.

If you place a sign on the property, go beyond a simple For Rent sign. Describe the unit, such as "2 Bedroom Apartment for Rent" or "For Rent: 3BR, 1½ Ba House." Inexpensive, customized signs can often be purchased at local sign shops.

#98. Should I offer incentives to attract better tenants?

Smart landlords often offer incentives to attract prospective tenants. Incentives can be reduced security deposits, one month of free rent, or rent reductions, such as $100 off each month's rent for the next six months.

New carpet might be a good incentive for some tenants. Others may prefer new appliances.

Allowing small pets without an additional security deposit can be a great incentive. Because so many landlords have a no-pets policy, allowing small pets could make your rental unit attractive to those that have a small dog or a cat.

One successful strategy for a landlord is to not collect more as security deposit when a tenant has a pet. Instead, simply charge a higher rent. The additional rent covers any damage, and unlike a security deposit that needs to be returned, the additional rent is the landlord's to keep. Pet damage is deducted from the security deposit. But by not attempting to collect an additional security deposit for the pet, this landlord's rental units remain occupied—and at a higher rent.

#99.   **How should I structure a rent-to-own deal?**

Some real estate investors purchase a property and then rent it with an option to buy contract. Landlords can also use this strategy.

The contract or lease includes additional terms. The property remains a rental, and rent is due to the landlord each month. However, at the time of the rental, an agreement is made between the landlord and the tenant that the property can be purchased for a specific price. That price cannot be changed by the property owner. For example, if both the landlord and the tenant agree the sales price is $150,000, the tenant can purchase the property for that amount at any time during the rental.

Often, these types of agreements include a credit for part of the rent to be applied to the purchase price. For example, a $200 monthly credit is applied each month to the agreed purchase price. After 12 months, the tenant would have a $2,400 credit (12 × $200). Instead of a $150,000 purchase price, the tenant could purchase the property for $147,600 ($150,000 minus the credit of $2,400).

Tenants that are attempting to purchase a property are likely to maintain it and not damage it.

#100.   **What is the difference between a lease purchase or option-to-buy versus a rent-to-own transaction?**

The differences can vary from state to state, but a rent-to-own transaction is simply a rental agreement with the option to purchase the property during the rental period for a specific, agreed sum. Often these types of agreements include a credit—a partial amount of the rent payment is applied toward the purchase price, reducing the amount each month that the property could be purchased. The tenant is under no obligation to purchase the property.

A lease purchase or option-to-buy is not a rental. Although the title to the property is not transferred, the occupant is required to purchase the property within a specific period or by a specific date.

If they fail to do so, they lose the property, including all down payment funds and equity. Although this may appear to be a rental, in reality, this type of arrangement is not. Of course, the occupant could walk away from the property and lose the equity.

Before entering into any kind of agreement such as this, you should consult with your lawyer and fully understand your duties and obligations of the contracts, and the differences between them.

#101. **Which utilities should I pay?**

The payment of utilities is something you must consider for each of your rental units. The utilities must be paid when due, by either you or your tenant.

Utilities include electric, gas, water, sewer, trash removal, and condominium or association fees. Heating oil might also be considered utilities.

If you are passing along any of the utility payments to your tenants, you must make sure that the utilities are paid on time. You may be held liable for any unpaid utilities.

If you have a multiunit rental property, any utility that is supplied to the multiple units should be paid by the landlord. For example, if the property does not have separated water service and water meters, but rather just a single water supply and one water meter, the landlord should pay for the water service.

#102. **What utilities should I require the tenant to pay?**

The tenant should pay consumption utilities, if it is practicable and possible. For example, water and electricity costs are based on the amount used. The more electricity or water consumed, the higher the bill will be.

As a landlord, it is difficult to determine what the likely monthly bill will be for consumption utilities. A "best guess" is all that can be determined. Adding that best guess into the monthly rent could be problematic if the tenant's usage is much higher than your estimate. That is why it is best to have the tenant pay the consumption utilities, when possible.

Fixed costs, such as sewerage service charges or trash removal, do not vary from month to month. It is always easier for the landlord to budget for these types of costs.

Landlords need to be careful when they require tenants to pay utilities. Local laws could allow the utility to cut off service to the property or require the property owner to pay the bill. A system needs to be in place to assure the utilities are paid. Some landlords receive the bill, forward the amount owed to the tenant, and require the tenant to pay the amount through the landlord. This assures the utility bill has been paid.

#103. Should I ever give my tenants "free rent" as part of their move-in?

The decision to offer free rent to your tenant is always up to you. It is common to allow a tenant to move in a few days early (especially at the end of the month) because the tenant must vacate his or her current residence before the end of the month. Whether you should charge for these few extra days is your decision.

Whether you charge rent or not for this short period, the lease should be prepared to include these few days. Occupancy should always include the actual dates the tenant has possession of the property. If you are giving free rent to the tenant for these days, indicate it on the lease.

The few days of free rent can often be considered good will toward your tenant. That doesn't mean a tenant won't try to take advantage of you later, but it could help by starting the landlord-tenant relationship on a friendly footing.

PART **3**

Managing the Property

TAKING CARE OF the property is an important part of being a landlord. Without a property, there is nothing to rent. The property is the investment, and it requires the maintenance and constant attention of the landlord. It often requires quick responses to solve problems when they occur. A hands-on approach is important, and this section helps landlords understand the best way to manage their rental properties.

#104.   **What is a move-in inspection?**

At the time the rental unit is ready to be turned over to the new tenant, a move-in inspection should be completed. The inspection should be part of the process. It is here where any deficiencies, damage, or problems are noted. For example, if the stove is scratched, that damage is noted on the inspection report. Both the tenant and the landlord should sign and date the report.

Prior to the arrival of the tenant at the property, the landlord should inspect the rental unit thoroughly. Obviously, the rental unit should be clean and in good condition. Successful landlords often photograph the unit. Using a small, "throwaway" camera, the condition of the rental unit is documented. There is no need to develop the film immediately. The camera is saved, and the film is only developed later, should there be a dispute about the move-in condition of the property. Because of the low cost of the disposable camera, it is considered good insurance to later prove damages caused by the tenant.

#105.   **How should a move-in inspection be conducted?**

The move-in inspection should always be a part of every rental. Based on what is and what is not recorded on the report, the ability to collect for damages caused by the tenant during the rental is determined.

The inspection report should include a report of each room and area rented to the tenant. Obvious defects, such as a spot on a carpet or a scratch on the wall, should be recorded on the report.

The more detailed the report, the better it is for both the landlord and tenant. Record everything that could be a deficiency.

Many landlords allow the tenant to complete the report and submit it several days after the tenancy begins. This allows the tenant time to find anything with the unit that may be considered damage.

In addition to being used as documentation as to what the condition is prior to the rental, compared to the condition when the tenant moves out, the move-in report also alerts the landlord as to what may need to be repaired or fixed. Some things may never be fixed, such as a scratch on a refrigerator, but other things may need immediate attention.

#106.   **What is a tenant orientation?**

Another part of the move-in process, the landlord should review and provide specific information with the tenant. The landlord should show the tenant how to adjust the heating and cooling controls. Any special instructions concerning any other amenity should also be given to the tenant.

Safety equipment should be pointed out to the tenant and checked. This includes smoke detectors and fire extinguishers. The landlord should demonstrate how to check to make certain these items are in working order.

Other important information should be given to the tenant. This includes contact information for utilities, schools, public services, and emergency services. Most landlords prepare an informational sheet that includes this type of information. It tells the tenant whom to call to get cable or telephone service, where to enroll a child in school, and so on.

Information for the tenant on how to contact the landlord is also provided.

#107.   **Can I restrict smoking in my rental unit?**

Yes. A ban on smoking in common areas is similar to other rules tenants typically must follow regarding the use of common areas, such as the hours for using the laundry facility or the requirement that an adult accompany children when using the pool.

It is also legal and valid for a landlord to ban smoking in individual rental units. Landlords have the legal right to set limits and rules on how a tenant may use rental property—for instance, by restricting guests, noise, and pets. A "no smoking" term is similar to a "no pets" restriction in the lease—another way for a landlord to protect his or her property.

A landlord is not unlawfully discriminating against smoking tenants or violating a smoker's fundamental right to privacy when banning smoking in common areas or individual rental units. Claims to the contrary have no legal basis.

#108. Am I allowed to have a "no pets" policy?

Yes, generally you can establish a "no pets" policy for your rental units. Your policy needs to be in writing. Most landlords include the "no pets" policy in their tenant's rules.

The only exception where a landlord cannot prohibit "pets" is for tenants with companion animals when prescribed by a licensed medical professional under the specific terms of the Americans with Disabilities Act.

Clever tenants may try to claim their pet is an emotional support animal. Because emotional support and service animals are not "pets," but rather are considered to be more like assistive aids such as wheelchairs, the law will generally require the landlord to make an exception to any "no pet" policy so that a tenant with a disability can fully use and enjoy their rented home.

#109. Am I permitted to have a no children policy?

Generally, no. It is a violation of law to set up a policy that discriminates against families. The law provides that you must rent to families with children, unless your property is exempt under specific federal regulations. The Fair Housing laws forbid landlords from discriminating in rental housing against persons based on their "familial status."

Familial status refers to children under the age of eighteen living with a parent or person having legal custody of such individuals. Familial status also applies to any person who is pregnant or in the process of securing legal custody of children under the age of eighteen.

According to HUD, housing for older persons is exempt from the prohibition against familial status discrimination if:

- The HUD Secretary has determined that it is specifically designed for and occupied by elderly persons under a federal, state, or local government program or
- It is occupied solely by persons who are sixty-two years of age or older or
- It houses at least one person who is fifty-five or older in at least 80 percent of the occupied units, and adheres to a policy that demonstrates intent to house persons who are fifty-five or older.

#110.   Can I limit the number of people that may live in the property?

Yes. You cannot discriminate against familial status, but you are not required to allow an unlimited number of persons to live within your rental unit.

The standard or norm is two persons per bedroom. The makeup of the family should not be used as the judgment as to whether or not to rent a unit. Rather, tenancy should be based on the total number of people, regardless of age, sex, or relationships to each other.

All adults (those over eighteen who are not the dependent children of a tenant) should be required to apply for tenancy, go through the approval process, and be added to the lease agreement. They should sign the lease, accepting the terms and conditions. This binds them contractually to specific duties and responsibilities. Many successful landlords require adults that live in their units more than two weeks to apply for tenancy and sign a lease agreement.

#111.   **What is the best way to collect the rent?**

The collection of the monthly rent is part of the process of operating a successful rental property enterprise. The rent is normally due on the first of each month. The most common method is for the tenant to send the rent payment to the landlord via the U.S. mail. Other landlords would rather stop at the property to pick up the payment.

The tenant should be willing and able to send the rent to the landlord by dropping a check in the mail. The check should be at the landlord's address on or before the due date. It is normal to allow a few days grace period, should the payment be held up in the mail. This is typically three to five days.

Other landlords routinely stop by their property to pick up the monthly rent. They often collect cash and issue a rent receipt to their tenant. They also use this opportunity to check on their property and to make sure the tenant is taking reasonable care of the property.

#112.   **What should I do when a rent payment is late?**

When rent is due and not received, the landlord should immediately notify the tenant in writing. A demand for the rent should be mailed to the tenant. Often, it is best to deliver a copy of the notice to the tenant by placing it in an envelope and taping the envelope on the main door of the premises.

Lease agreements include provisions as to what penalties are assessed to the tenant should the rent payment be late. Usually these penalties are only invoked after a grace period, which is typically three to five days after the due date.

There should be no doubt that the rent is overdue and expected to be paid immediately, with any overdue or late payment charges.

Your policy regarding demanding late rent should be automatic and uniform. Do not give special or preferential treatment to one tenant over another. If your grace period is five days, on the sixth day send the late notice demand to any tenants that have not paid the rent.

#113. How much tolerance should I give a late-paying renter?

You should give zero-tolerance to a tenant that is late in paying the rent. The more tolerance you give, the more likely the tenant will use it to their advantage. If you allow a tenant to be ten days late in paying the rent, then you should expect all rent payments to be late.

When the rent is due, you should expect it and do everything possible to see that it has been paid. If it has not been paid by the established grace period, send a notice of late payment.

If it is still not paid, prepare the eviction notice to the tenant. The eviction notice—and when it can be sent—varies among locations. Some will not consider it valid unless the rent is more than fifteen or twenty-one days past due. Determine what the law is for your area. Send the notice as soon as you are allowed to do so. Send your eviction notice via both certified and regular mail.

#114. Am I allowed to collect late fees on past due rent?

Usually a landlord is allowed to collect late fees on rent that has not been paid. Local laws and the lease agreements determine the amount of a late fee that can be collected. The purpose of the penalty or late fee is to assure the tenant pays the rent on time.

Don't allow a tenant to be late and forgive the late fees when the rent is finally paid.

Typically, a tenant who fails to pay a late fee cannot be evicted on a nonpayment of rent notice. In many jurisdictions, a tenant who receives a notice for nonpayment of rent can keep from being evicted by paying only the rent and not the late fee during the notice period. A landlord is not permitted to deduct the late fee from this rent payment and then claim that a portion of the rent is still due.

Tenants who have not paid late fees can be evicted, but usually on a thirty-day notice, even if all rent has been paid.

#115. Should I accept partial payments of the rent that is due?

This is tricky, and the answer varies greatly among jurisdictions. In some locales, accepting a partial payment does not affect the landlord's ability to collect remaining rent or surrenders the right to evict. In other jurisdictions, courts have ruled that accepting partial rent payments stops the ability to evict for unpaid rent for the month the partial payment was received.

It is difficult not to accept some payment—rather than no money— from a tenant. However, in doing so, a landlord may be waiving important rights. Much of this has been determined by local court decisions. The only way to determine what is right in your area is to consult with your real estate attorney.

#116. Where can a landlord get help with rent collection?

Every jurisdiction has some judicial method for collecting unpaid rent and handling evictions of tenants that do not pay rent. No one expects a landlord to continue to rent a property to someone who does not pay rent.

The judicial system, often a form of a small claims court, is the best source of help to the landlord. The court will have rules and guidelines to follow. As long as you follow the steps properly and can prove your case through the proper paperwork that you produce, you can easily win your case. If the tenant cannot prove payment, the landlord will win and get his property back.

Don't try creative ideas to help collect your rent. Things like removing doors or locks, turning off heat, or scheduling repairs that make the unit uninhabitable (even if the rent has not been paid) do not work. In many areas, such schemes are likely to have a judgment entered against the landlord and in favor of the tenant. You could end up owing money to a tenant that owes you for unpaid rent.

#117. **Are there any creative ways to get the rent paid on time?**

Some late-paying tenants can be handled with an incentive. One technique that has worked for other successful landlords is to offer a rent discount to any tenant that pays their rent on or before the day it is due. It works this way: you rent a property for $815. However, if a tenant pays the rent on or before the 25th of each month, they are entitled to a $25 discount. In other words, they rent the property for $790. Their rent check can't bounce, and it must be in your hands by the first of the month to qualify. Inexperienced property owners that use this technique are often amazed what a tenant will do to enjoy a rent reduction.

This incentive need not actually cost you anything. You could build a late fee into the base rent. By paying on or before the first, the tenant gets a "discount," or they avoid the late fee, depending on your perspective. If rent remains unpaid, additional late fees could apply.

#118. **Should I keep a copy of all rent checks received from a tenant?**

Good recordkeeping is essential to the success of profitably renting property. Maintaining meticulous records of rent receipts from tenants is essential.

One easy way to maintain the rent payment record is to make a copy of each rent check received before it is deposited in your bank account. The copy of the tenant's check is placed in their file folder.

If rent is received as cash, a copy of the rent receipt issued to the tenant should be placed in their file folder.

Some jurisdictions require that when rent is paid in cash, the landlord must issue a rent receipt. Good business dictates that you do this. If you don't, a disgruntled tenant might decide you pocketed the rent without reporting the income on your taxes. They could easily report you to the IRS, regardless of how legitimate your rental business may be.

#119. Am I allowed to charge a fee for a bad or insufficient funds check given to me by a tenant for rent?

Usually a tenant's check that has been returned from the bank marked as nonsufficient funds (NSF) incurs a fee for you. Most jurisdictions allow a landlord to collect a fee when this occurs. The amount of the fee should be included in the lease or the rules.

In addition to the returned check fee, the rent should be considered unpaid, and demand for the rent should be issued immediately. Late fees, for the unpaid rent, should also be demanded.

Keep in mind that bad checks can happen to anyone, and for any number of reasons. From sloppy handling of funds to someone issuing a bad check to a tenant, there could be little intent to give you a bad check for the rent.

Be flexible and understanding when you receive a bad check from a tenant. Most tenants will try to fix the problem promptly. Only those that do not intend to pay the rent will not try to remedy a bad check.

#120. What should a landlord do if a tenant declares bankruptcy?

Today's bankruptcy laws allow a landlord to evict a tenant from the rental unit. As of October 17, 2005, when the new bankruptcy laws took effect, a key change is that filing for bankruptcy no longer delays or stops eviction actions.

The federal Bankruptcy Abuse Prevention and Consumer Protection Act of 2005 provides that if a landlord has already filed an eviction action against a tenant and obtained a judgment of possession—an order of the court evicting the tenant—the tenant's subsequent bankruptcy filing will not automatically stop the eviction.

Different court rules apply if the tenant files for bankruptcy before the landlord obtains an eviction judgment. Filing for bankruptcy does not prevent a tenant from being evicted. The law requires the landlord to get permission from the Bankruptcy Court before proceeding with the eviction.

Therefore the filing of a bankruptcy action by the tenant may slow down the eventual eviction, but it cannot stop it.

#121. **Can I raise the rent during the lease period?**

Generally, rent can only be raised during the rental period according to the terms and conditions of the lease agreement. Unless the lease agreement permits the rent to be increased, the rent will remain the same throughout the rental period.

Many standard residential leases are for a one-year period, and then convert to a month-to-month rental agreement. At that time, the rent can be raised every thirty days.

Other rental leases have a provision that renew for another year, under all the terms and conditions of the previous, except the rent amount. The lease allows the rent to be increased. Sometimes it is restricted to no more than a certain percentage, such as 5 percent.

The lease agreement will provide the answers as to whether the rent can be raised during the rental period. The general rule is that rent cannot be raised during the first year, but can be raised after that period. The exception is a month-to-month rental, when the rent can be raised after giving the tenant thirty days notice of the rent increase.

#122.   **How often can a landlord raise the rent?**

The lease agreement determines how often the landlord is permitted to raise the rent. Practically speaking, rent is usually only raised once a year. Doing so more often can cause a tenant to move.

Always look to the lease agreement to determine how the rent can be raised. It is typical that rent cannot be raised during the first year of tenancy, unless permitted in the lease.

The smallest rent increase can cause a tenant to move. A tenant might decide to move because the rent was raised $20 a month. Even though it will cost the tenant more than $240 to move, they see that as a more reasonable alternative than paying the extra $20 each month.

Sometimes, the best way to raise the rent is to do so when the tenant requests something that is an added expense. For example, if a tenant requests that you provide a new refrigerator, that might be the best time to raise the monthly rent. The rise in rent can only be done if permitted by the terms and conditions of the lease agreement.

#123.   **What is the most common reason landlords do not start the eviction process?**

Landlords often do not start the eviction process because they are afraid of vacancy and turnover costs. Rather than evict, landlords tolerate more than they should from a tenant.

It does take time and money to turn over a rental unit. After a unit is vacated, it often needs cleaning, painting, and repairs. Then the landlord must advertise and market the property, process an applicant, and finally get the new tenant in the property. This takes time, and no rent is being collected during the process.

When a tenant does not voluntarily vacate, it can take several months for the legal process to proceed. Some tenants, knowing they are being evicted, will remain in the premises but not pay any rent or any other expenses.

Successful landlords know that when a tenant goes bad, it is time to cut the losses and get the tenant out of the property. Time will not make a bad tenant better. It will only make a bad tenant worse.

#124.   What are the standard rules for tenants?

All landlords should have rules for their tenants. The rules of occupancy vary and are often based on the type of the property being rented.

Standard rules include such things as being quiet from 10 P.M. to 7 A.M., removal of trash, and prohibitions on certain things, such as waterbeds, motorcycles, or pets. Cleanliness, pets, and noise are often the areas where most rules are created. It may amaze many new landlords as to how slovenly some people will live, preferring squalor and filth to tidiness.

Rules generally are established to protect the property and to make certain the tenancy of the property is not a problem for others. Some rules should also be posted on the property. For example, if there is a common laundry, rules about its use should be posted clearly. Common rules such as, "Laundry is not to be used after 10 P.M. or before 7 A.M." should be posted so all tenants can abide by it.

#125.   Should the tenant rules be made part of the lease?

It is common to include rules with the lease. Many leases include a condition that the tenant will comply with the rules the landlord establishes for the premises.

Rules should always be in writing. Attach them as part of the lease, and it is best to have all tenants sign a copy of the rules, acknowledging they have received them and agree to follow them.

Often rules need to be changed or modified. When that occurs, you should always provide an updated copy to your tenants. Be sure to date each version of your rules.

Your rules should be easy to understand and comprehend. All rules should be specific. Don't include anything that is so generic that it has no meaning or enforcement. A rule such as "every tenant should act proper" means nothing, and could not be enforced. Rules should be specific, clear, and unambiguous, such as "Pets are not permitted on the property at any time."

#126. How should scheduled or routine maintenance be completed?

One of the dynamics of being a landlord is that the property must be properly maintained. Throughout the year, it will be necessary to enter a rental until to perform maintenance.

You (or your representative) cannot enter the premises without prior notification to the tenant. Most leases include this provision and require a minimum of twenty-four hours notice prior to entrance for nonemergency purposes. The twenty-four hours notice can be by telephone or written notice. Some landlords will call the tenant, while others will place a notice on the door notifying of the scheduled maintenance.

It is always best to accomplish as much as possible when entering the unit for scheduled maintenance. For example, you might be changing the filter in the heating or air conditioning unit. At the same time, you might check the fire extinguisher and test the smoke detectors. It is better to minimize the maintenance trips as much as possible.

#127. When can a landlord enter a rental unit?

A tenant has the right to enjoy the peaceful use of their rental unit. Unlawful entry could result in a lawsuit claiming an invasion of privacy.

All jurisdictions grant the landlord the right to enter a rental unit in emergencies. Common sense would dictate when this is necessary. An emergency is not to paint a wall or check to see if a fire extinguisher needs recharging. The smell of gas or leaking water would be classified as an emergency situation.

Landlords can enter the rented premises only:

- To make needed repairs (or to determine whether repairs are necessary)
- In cases of emergency
- To show the property to prospective new tenants or purchasers

Some states also allow landlords or property managers the right of entry during a tenant's extended absence (which is usually defined as seven days or more) to maintain the property as necessary and to inspect for damage and needed repairs. A landlord may not enter just to check up on the tenant and the rental property.

#128. Can a tenant give permission to enter the rental unit?

Yes, a tenant can grant permission to the landlord at any time to enter the rented premises. The tenant can waive the advanced notice requirement.

Those states that regulate the landlord's access require landlords to provide advance notice before entering a rental unit. For the most part, the advance notice is twenty-four hours for nonemergency entrance.

Usually a landlord is permitted to knock on a door and ask permission to enter (if the tenant is at the premises). The landlord cannot enter without first asking and being granted permission by the tenant.

The problem is that the tenant can always claim intimidation or assert some other claim against the landlord. It is for this reason that the landlord should not enter the premises without advanced, written notice, whenever possible.

#129. What are the best ways to handle emergency repairs?

Eventually, an emergency situation will occur at the property. The tenant must know what to do. For example, when a pipe breaks and water is leaking, the tenant needs to know where and how to shut off the water, and then whom to call.

Many successful landlords provide a list of what is and what is not an emergency. While no heat is considered an emergency, no cable service is not an emergency.

Landlords should provide an emergency phone number to all tenants. When they do not, it is likely the tenant will take matters into their own hands and present the landlord with an expensive repair bill. For example, a cracked and leaking toilet needs repair, and it is unreasonable to expect a tenant to go for any period without a toilet. Without telling them beforehand what to do, you can expect them to call a plumber to get it repaired.

#130. Should I charge for accidental lockouts?

You can charge your tenant a fee for an accidental lockout. For legal reasons, always call it a fee and not rent. Bill for the fee immediately. Establish the fee you will assess for lockouts. This is a good item to include on your rules, making it clear what you will charge should the tenant be locked out of their rental unit.

Often daytime lockouts are not charged. Lockouts that occur during the evening or weekends are assessed the fee. Some landlords establish a policy that the first lockout is free, but subsequent lockouts are billable.

Some tenants can be tricky in trying to avoid the lockout fee. When the landlord charges a lockout fee, a tenant might break a window or crack a doorjamb. The tenant would rather make the landlord think a tempted thief caused damage rather than the tenant carelessly locked the keys in their rental unit.

#131. **If a tenant pays the rent but breaks the rules, can the tenant be evicted?**

Yes. Paying rent is only one of the many obligations of the tenant. The lease will often establish other requirements on the part of the tenant, such as obeying rules.

A landlord may discover the tenant has dangerous materials on the premises. The landlord can begin the eviction process immediately to get the tenant and the dangerous materials out of the property.

Any kind of illegal activity, possession of prohibited items, and breaches of rules are always grounds for eviction. The landlord must be able to prove their position. Often a simple photograph or video is more than sufficient evidence to prove to a judge that the tenant breached the rules. For example, showing a judge a picture of puppies in the rental unit is sufficient to prove the tenant has broken the no-pets policy.

When a tenant breaks rules, don't hesitate to begin the eviction process. Never threaten to evict. Simply proceed with the eviction. By commencing eviction proceedings, the tenant will need either to comply or leave the premises.

#132. **Can tenants drill holes to install electronics and other similar items?**

The landlord can certainly demand and expect that a tenant not cause any damage to the rental unit. The landlord can certainly prohibit a tenant from drilling holes to run wires, install a satellite dish, or install wall brackets for big screen TVs.

In reality, tenants will drill the holes and install many of the luxury electronic items they want and will enjoy. They will install and use speaker systems, computers, big screen high definition television sets, and other such items. Whenever possible, it may be best to allow such installations, as long as they are done professionally. Allowing such installations may create a happier and contented renter. There may be items that a landlord cannot allow to be installed, but other items could be installed without difficulty or problems.

When approving the installation, always put the approval in writing. Include the condition in which a professional installer must complete the installation, and that the tenant is responsible for any damage. Make sure the tenant accepts the terms of your approval by signing a copy of the letter and returning it to you.

#133. How should I plan and handle major repairs or renovations?

Ideally, major repairs or renovations should be completed during a turnover period. When the property is vacant, it is easier to get workers in and repairs made.

However, it is not always possible to schedule work during vacancies. Budgets, contractor's schedules, weather, and other factors can make it nearly impossible to complete work within a given time.

It is best to keep good communications going between the landlord and the tenant. For example, the landlord might inform the tenant, "Next year, the building is scheduled for a new roof." As the time gets closer, the landlord might state that a new roof will be installed "sometime in the spring." The next communication might be something like, "The roof will be replaced during the month of May." By doing so, when the contractors arrive in mid-May, it will not be a surprise to the tenant.

#134. **What should I do when repairs do not go as planned?**

It is not uncommon for something to not go as hoped, especially when repairs, workers, and renovations are mixed together. The problems are multiplied when the rental unit is uninhabitable.

Always take care of your tenant and the tenant's needs. If the basics (electric, plumbing, heat) are not working, it might be necessary to put the tenant up in a motel room. If it's more of an inconvenience, show your compassion by giving the tenant a credit off their next month's rent payment. You can also pay for a meal or two by giving the tenant a gift card at a nearby restaurant. These small gestures can eliminate massive problems later.

Make certain that workers and contractors realize that they must complete the work on time so your rental units are habitable and your tenants can stay there. Closely monitor the progress of the work being completed.

#135. **Should I ever allow my tenants to do repairs or renovations?**

Landlords are often faced with a request from a tenant to do certain work for a reduction in rent. Some tenants request the landlord pay for the materials, and volunteer to do the work necessary to complete the upgrade, repair, or minor renovations.

Common requests are for paint and materials. The tenant will paint a room if the landlord will pay for the paint, brushes, and other incidental items.

Requests can vary, from installing a dishwasher or adding a center island in a kitchen to adding screen doors or storage units. At issue is how much it will cost the landlord, if the requested repair or renovation will be professionally completed, and if it will devalue the property in any way.

Allowing the tenant to complete a project often extends good will and keeps the tenant content. Allowing the tenant to paint a room or wall seldom causes huge problems. At worse, when the tenant vacates, the room would need to be repainted. To eliminate many problems, a landlord purchases the paint so it is a color acceptable to the landlord.

#136.   Is it wise to allow tenants to paint the rental unit?

There is no set rule about painting. If the rental unit needs painting due to ordinary wear and tear, the responsibility is the landlord's. If the need for painting is the fault of the tenant because of damage, then the tenant is responsible.

The condition of the paint can make a property "habitable" or "inhabitable." When the paint chips or peels, the landlord must correct the condition.

When a tenant wants to paint to make the rental unit more attractive, you might consider buying the paint (probably no more than $30 for a small apartment) if the tenant will do the painting. Sometimes, landlords purchase partial cans of paint at yard or garage sales for touch-up or small rooms.

When you allow a tenant to do the painting, you are taking a risk in assuming that they know how to paint properly. Will your tenant remove the electrical outlet covers and switch plates? Sloppy painting can become a problem.

You should always maintain control over the paint color. If you don't, you could end up with wall colors that will require much repainting when your tenant leaves.

#137. **Does it make sense to expect or require a tenant to perform maintenance work, like grass cutting and snow removal, as part of the rental agreement?**

Sometimes, the best way to make sure exterior maintenance is completed is for the landlord to do the work. However, many successful landlords do require their tenants to do certain maintenance work around the premises.

It is always best to include the responsibilities and duties of the tenant in the lease agreement. It should be clearly indicated and spelled out in unambiguous terms. For example: "Tenant agrees to mow the rear yard weekly (or more often) so as to maintain the grass no more than two inches in height."

In some locales, local laws or ordinances require snow removal from sidewalks. If the tenant fails to do this work, the property owner is likely to be held responsible by the local authorities. Be sure that if you delegate this type of work to a tenant that the work is done on time and as agreed. You must comply with local laws, and if the tenant does not do the work as required, you may be held legally responsible.

#138. **What is the best way to handle appliance problems?**

Most residential rental units include the use of several appliances. It is common that a stove be included with a rental. Many units include the use of a refrigerator, washer and dryer, dishwasher, and garbage disposal.

The more appliances in the rental unit, the more they need to be maintained and kept working.

In today's world, many appliances are disposable. Rather than pay for costly repairs, the appliance is simply replaced by a new model. Landlords usually purchase less expensive models for their rental units, and some purchase used appliances. Scratched and dented appliances (usually discounted because of the damage) are often attractive purchases to the landlord.

Some repairs are easy for anyone to fix. For example, if a heating element on an electric stove needs replacement, it is a simple matter of purchasing a new one, unplugging the old one, and plugging in the new element.

#139.   What should I do about moisture problems?

Moisture problems can cause serious and extensive damage. Never ignore moisture in a rental unit. The problem with moisture is that it can help mold cultivate. Mold should not be permitted to grow and multiply indoors. When this happens, health problems can occur and building materials, goods, and furnishings may be damaged. Mold only needs a few simple things to grow and multiply:

- Moisture
- Nutrients
- A suitable place to grow

Of these, controlling excess moisture is the key to preventing and stopping indoor mold growth.

Excessive moisture can also cause wood rot and create other structural damage. A leaking pipe, roof, or other opening that allows water to enter a residential property, and is not cleaned up, will only get worse in time.

Don't ignore moisture problems. Give them the highest priority. As soon as a problem is discovered, solve it by removing the source of the moisture. What might be nothing more than a small amount of caulk or a tightening of a pipe joint could prevent thousands of dollars of damage or personal injury claims.

#140. **How do I comply with the lead paint disclosure?**

Older residential properties could have lead paint in them. Lead was a common ingredient added to paint for decades prior to 1974. Many of those homes with lead paint still exist.

Over the recent years, government regulations and policies require the elimination or abatement of specific hazardous conditions. The law holds the landlord responsible for any hazards on your property.

Because of the danger to your tenants—especially children—a property with lead paint is a particular problem. Lead-based paint cannot simply be scraped off and the surface repainted. Strict environmental regulations must be followed. In some locales, the property must have the lead paint properly removed before it can be rented. The best way to eliminate any potential lawsuit is to de-lead the property, regardless of state or local laws.

The federal government banned lead as an ingredient in paint in 1974. However, owing to the existing stock of paint that may have already been in existence, the government has determined that any housing built prior to 1978 may contain lead-based paint. If the property was built before 1978, the government requires landlords to furnish tenants with a copy of a booklet called *Protect Your Family from Lead in Your Home.* It is available online at *www.hud.gov.*

#141. **What do you do when a tenant simply abandons the property?**

In most areas, the tenant is considered to have abandoned the dwelling if the tenant is absent from the dwelling, without notice to the owner, for over seven continuous days, if the absence occurs after rent for the unit is delinquent. If the tenant abandons the dwelling unit, the landlord is entitled to take immediate possession of the rental unit.

When abandonment occurs, the landlord does not need to file an eviction action with the local court. Since the tenant has left, the possession of the property returns to the landlord.

The landlord should take immediate action to protect against any claim by the tenant. Send both a notice by regular mail and certified mail to the tenant declaring that the rental unit has been abandoned, and you are taking possession. Request a forwarding address from the postal service. Also, send the notice to the person to notify in case of emergency that was provided by the tenant during the application process.

#142. When does a tenant lose ownership of personal property left at a rental property?

Each jurisdiction has established its own rules regarding the abandonment of personal property. When the personal property was actually abandoned by its owner is always subject to legal interpretation.

Although laws differ, once the rental unit has been abandoned, the landlord must usually send some kind of notice of abandonment to all known addresses of the tenant. Often, laws require the landlord to post a notice of abandonment on the door of the premises. If the tenant does not contact the landlord within a specific number of days, then the property can be entered, personal property cleared, and the premises rented. The personal property usually must be stored, and if not claimed within a specific amount of time, can be sold. The proceeds can usually be used to pay for moving and storage costs, damages, and owed rent.

When a landlord takes over control of personal property, it should always be inventoried and photographed before being moved. What might seem to be junk or trash could later be claimed as expensive chattel.

#143. **When the tenant abandons the rental unit, what should the landlord do with the property the tenant has left on the premises?**

In most jurisdictions, when the tenant abandons the rental unit, the landlord does not need to acquire a lien on the tenant's personal property. Although the laws vary among jurisdictions, before disposing of the tenant's personal property, the landlord must:

- Place the entire tenant's personal property in storage for thirty days, if the property has been on the premises for not less than thirty days.
- Provide written notice to the tenant of landlord's intent to dispose of the personal property on a date not less than thirty days from the date of the notice. The written notice should include a telephone number and address where the resident can reasonably contact the landlord prior to the disposal date.
- Deliver the notice of intent to dispose of personal property to the tenant or send it by first class mail to the resident's last known address.

#144. **What should I do if the tenant's Notice of Abandonment is returned to me?**

If your notice to your former tenant is returned by the postal service as undeliverable, you should send the notice to any other address the tenant provided, including the address of their place of employment, or to a family member or emergency contact. You want to be able to prove that you have been more than reasonable and prudent in attempting to contact your former tenant.

The landlord can dispose of the abandoned personal property if the tenant has not responded accordingly. Before doing so, photograph it to show its value should claim be made against you by a former tenant.

The landlord may charge the tenant a reasonable storage fee for any time that the landlord provided storage for the former resident's personal property and the prevailing rate of moving fees. In most jurisdictions, the landlord may require payment of storage and moving costs prior to the release of the property.

#145. **Should I spend time and money to track down a tenant that has skipped and still owes rent?**

There are many factors to consider before hunting down a disappearing tenant. First, how much money is owed to you? If the amount is small, it may not be economically prudent to chase your former tenant. If the amount is substantial, it may make more sense to pursue your claim.

Second, where did the tenant go? If the former tenant crossed state lines, it becomes more difficult to serve legal processes, and if a judgment is obtained, to collect it. If the tenant has disappeared, it is impossible to serve process and collect any court ordered payment.

Many times, landlords that are owed money from former tenants turn the owed amount over to a professional collection agency. The collection agency pursues the former tenant and can enter the amount owed onto the credit report. This technique may make the tenant work out some type of payment plan to clear the collection on the credit report.

#146. **Can I evict a tenant for something other than nonpayment of rent?**

Yes. A tenant can be evicted for any legitimate reason. Violation of other terms of the rental agreement or infractions of your rules are reasons enough to evict a tenant.

The eviction process is the same as when the tenant has not paid rent. The problem is that an eviction for other than nonpayment of rent may not be as easy to prove. When a tenant does not pay rent, the landlord will always win the case and get an eviction judgment. For other eviction reasons, the landlord might be held responsible for damages caused to the tenant.

Always put everything in writing. For a rule violation, write the tenant a letter. A second violation should be stronger, with a demand to obey rules. It should also include notification that eviction will be commenced if the tenant does not comply with your demand to follow all rules.

Of course, you need to keep copies of your correspondence. You must be able to show a judge that you notified the tenant of the problem, warned them, and gave them a chance to comply.

#147. **What should I do when a tenant violates a no-pets policy?**

In some jurisdictions, landlords may not be allowed to evict tenants just because they have pets. Laws have been passed making it illegal to discriminate against people who have a pet.

In the United States, a judge ruled against the managers of a California apartment community that had a no-pets policy. The judge decided the policy violated the Fair Housing Act when the property manager attempted to evict a disabled tenant because he had a cat. The tenant's physician said the cat served a therapeutic purpose and therefore, in the opinion of the judge, the apartment manager failed to make a "reasonable accommodation."

Yet in other jurisdictions, failing to enforce a no-pets policy is problematic. In Maryland, a mother sued a landlord for not enforcing a no-pets clause in a lease, after a pit bull attacked and killed a visiting child. The trial court found the landlord liable and awarded $6 million in damages.

#148.   **What is the eviction process?**

Eviction is a legal term. It is a court action requiring the tenant to vacate the premises, and returning it to the landlord. Each jurisdiction has its own process of evicting a tenant.

A tenant can voluntarily move. After receiving the landlord's notice that eviction will occur, the tenant may decide to vacate. When the tenant does not voluntarily turn over the rental unit to the landlord, then the legal process must begin.

Different jurisdictions have established different rules or procedures. Some may require a Notice to Quit, while others require an eviction complaint be filed in a small claims court. Whatever the procedure is, the landlord must follow it.

A landlord is always prohibited from illegally evicting a tenant without a court order. Landlords cannot lock out a tenant, remove doors to the property, or shut off utilities to the rental unit. Landlords have no legal authority to remove a tenant or property from a rental unit. If a landlord does so, the tenant has the right to file a lawsuit against the landlord and will likely win a judgment in his favor.

#149.   **What is "normal wear and tear"?**

The term "normal wear and tear" is vague and means different things to different people. Normal wear and tear includes things such as wall paint. A tenant does not cause the paint to fade and would not be responsible for the faded paint when the landlord decides to repaint.

Damages are actual things in the rental unit that the tenant or the tenant's guests actually break—such as breaking a window or making a hole in the wall.

Some examples of normal wear and tear are:

- Broken plumbing pipes, unless it is clear the tenant damaged them

- Dirty or dusty blinds
- Dust in the apartment
- Faded paint
- Furniture marks in carpet
- Hole or ding in a wall from missing doorstop

Some examples of damage (and not wear and tear) are:

- Animal stains
- Broken doors or windows
- Burn marks caused by an iron, cigar, or cigarette
- Clogged drains caused by misuse of sinks or toilets
- Eliminating flea infestations caused by the tenant's animals
- Holes in walls from hanging pictures
- Larger gouges on walls
- Missing or broken blinds or curtains
- Removal of decals on walls, appliances, cabinets, and other surfaces
- Smoke damage from smoking or burning candles
- Tears in the carpet

#150. Can I charge a tenant by deducting it from the security deposit for leaving trash, dirt, and filth in the rental unit?

Yes, a landlord is permitted to charge a tenant for the removal of trash and the cost of cleaning beyond normal conditions. The best way for the landlord to protect against claims of overcharging for trash and dirt cleanup is to document the condition with photographs or video.

Mounds of trash and garbage, abandoned furniture, and worthless household items left behind by a tenant should be discarded. The reasonable cost of removal and disposal should be charged to the tenant and deducted from the security deposit by the landlord.

There is a difference between filth and ordinary dirt. A carpet or a tile floor that needs cleaning is not damaged. Landlords should expect to clean a rental unit during the turnover process from one tenant to the next. Only charge for the excessive dirt or filth that must be cleaned from the rental unit.

#151.   How do I calculate tenant-caused damages?

Always be reasonable and prudent with any damages caused by the tenant. Always keep in mind that you must be able to explain and defend your charges in a small claims court proceeding. Charging a former tenant $150 for a nail hole in a wall is likely to be considered excessive.

One of the most common methods for calculating the deduction for replacement costs is to prorate the total cost of replacement. This is done so that the tenant pays only for the remaining useful life of the item that was damaged or destroyed.

Suppose a tenant has damaged beyond repair a four-year-old carpet that had a life expectancy of five years, and a replacement carpet of similar quality would cost $500. It is unreasonable to demand the tenant to pay $500. The landlord should charge only $100 for the one year's worth of use that would have remained if the tenant had not damaged the carpet. Be sure to document and explain all such calculations.

#152.   How do I calculate cleanup costs?

Successful landlords often have an established price list of cleanup charges that is provided to the tenant during the move-in process. The prices encourage the tenant to clean up when they vacate the rental unit.

Remember first that you should only charge for excessive and not routine cleanup of a rental unit. You should expect to tidy or clean a rental unit during the turnover process. Dusting or cleaning blinds, washing floors, cleaning a bathroom, or scrubbing the kitchen are expected. Don't try to charge the previous tenant for cleanup just because the rental unit was not left in a "spotless" condition. Only charge for excessive cleaning that must be done before the unit could be rented.

If you have a cleanup, turnover, or maintenance person that submits a bill for the service, it is easier to claim a specific amount than an arbitrary charge you write on a paper. If you do not have a service, you can use a reasonable per-hour charge to calculate cleanup.

#153. **How do I withhold part of the security deposit for damages?**

During the inspection after the tenant has vacated the rental unit, detailed notes should be included on a written report. You should take photographs of any damage.

Ignore minor blemishes, dents, or scuffs. Marks in the carpet from furniture are not damage. Dirt that can be easily cleaned should also not be considered damage. However, all of these findings should be documented. Even if you are not going to charge for scuffmarks on a wall—probably caused by moving furniture—write it down on your inspection report. When completed, prepare a list of charges based on the actual damages.

#154. **How long do I have to refund all or part of the security deposit?**

Local or state laws direct how long the tenant's security deposit is to be held by the landlord, and when the security deposit must be returned. Some laws require that the security deposit be held in an interest-bearing trust account in a bank or savings and loan. Other jurisdictions may not have any requirement as to how long the security deposit must be retained by the landlord.

Most laws pertaining to security deposits include how long a landlord has to return the security deposit to the tenant, less any legitimate deductions for tenant-caused damages. Generally, the deposit must be returned within thirty days, but the time exact time varies among different jurisdictions.

Landlords should return the security deposit as soon as possible. Include a list of deductions, and include a detailed explanation of the deductions applied to the security deposit. Be fair and reasonable with any charges.

#155. **When does it make sense to hire a property manager?**

A property manager turns your rental property into a turnkey investment, meaning that all you do is cash your rent checks. All the work—from finding tenants to handling emergency service calls—is handled by the property manager.

There are professional property management companies in most areas. Many times, they are a division or part of a local real estate brokerage firm.

There is little for the landlord to do once the property manager is engaged. The property manager will handle complaints, develop and enforce rules, provide legally tested lease or rental agreements, minimize vacancies, and do the work necessary to manage the property.

A property manager eliminates the daily management responsibility of running and operating a rental property. Rental managers make sense to landlords that want hands-off operations.

#156. **How much does a property manager cost?**

Property management services vary among locales and so does the cost. Years ago, most property management fees for residential property were set at 5 percent. Today, the fees can be anything from 2 to 10 percent of the rent or income collected. The property management fees vary greatly and depend on the services provided. Sometimes, the fee is also determined by the age of the property.

Older properties, which require more maintenance and attention, cost the landlord more for management.

The amount of service the landlord wants can determine the percentage or fees charged by the property manager. Some of the typical services include:

- Repairs and maintenance for occupancy
- Advertising and marketing
- Screening applicants, including application and credit verification
- Preparation of all lease documents
- Rent collection and disbursement
- Maintenance and twenty-four-hour emergency repair service
- Income and expense report for clients
- Management of accounts payable
- Compliance with all housing regulations

Property managers will require a property management agreement to be signed by the landlord. The agreement will specify the amount of the fee, the services to be provided, and the length of the agreement.

#157. What can I do to make my property more attractive to prospective tenants?

People often rent property based on their first impressions. Prospective tenants have pretty much decided whether they want to live somewhere before they even get out of their car. Whether they will rent your unit often depends on their first impression of your property.

One of the best ways to get more rent and better quality tenants is to make your rental property look as if it ought to rent for more money. Some of the things you can do to improve the first impression of your rental unit include:

- Add a built-in dishwasher
- Add a washer and dryer
- Always make your property look crisp and clean from the street
- Clean up the yard, plant flowers, and trim shrubs
- Give the tenant some kind of private, outside space, if possible
- Hang drapes and curtains
- Install a range
- Install a refrigerator
- Plant fruit trees and give the fruit to the tenants
- Shine everything that is supposed to shine or sparkle
- Wax the floors

#158. **What should I do about keeping the outside of the property maintained?**

Consider these items:

- Keep painted surfaces fresh with a good coat of paint.
- Always keep the property clean and litter-free.
- Detail the front entrance. Add those little touches that add class and style to your property. Front doors should have a solid and well-crafted light. Don't choose plastic over a more stylish, metal lamp.
- Be sure the property's street number is clearly visible from the street. Use stylish numbers (usually brass or ceramic) over cheap, inexpensive stick-ons.
- Make the front door sparkle by keeping it clean, scrubbed, and looking new.
- Add flower boxes and keep seasonal flowers growing in them.

- If the front of the property includes grass, keep it fertilized so it is green and looking healthy. Fix any dirt spots by planting grass seed.
- Trim shrubs and trees, and keep them maintained and trimmed.

Be fussy over the appearance of your property. Always take the extra effort to maintain the outside of your property. Don't allow it to deteriorate or look slovenly.

PART 4

Legal Issues

THE GOVERNMENT HAS stepped in and created all kinds of laws to control rental properties and landlords. This has occurred at all levels of government—both federal and state governments have enacted hundreds of laws. Many local governments have also enacted laws that control rental properties and their owners. Sometimes, it seems like a maze of complicated laws. This section of the book, while not intended to be a substitute for professional legal advice, will guide you through the various laws that affect you as a landlord.

#159. **What federal laws must I know?**

There are various federal laws that landlords must know. Federal law prohibits discrimination in housing and the rental market. The Federal Fair Housing and the Civil Rights Act include criminal and civil penalties for those that violate the law. The Federal Fair Housing Act of 1968 makes it illegal for a landlord to discriminate because of a person's race, sex, national origin, or religion.

Hundreds of landlords have been fined and debarred from doing business with the federal government because of failing to provide safe and decent housing for the poor, while enriching themselves on taxpayer-funded subsidies. Federal law also makes it illegal to advertise or make any statement that indicates a limitation or preference based on race, color, national origin, religion, sex, familial status, or handicap.

HUD publishes extensive guides and information for landlords to assist in compliance with federal laws. The information is available on HUD's website at *www.hud.gov*.

#160. **What state laws must I know?**

Each state has enacted extensive laws that control landlord and tenant relationships. These laws control renting, the rights of both parties, the handling of security deposits, and eviction processes. The best source of local law information is always your attorney.

State laws also place responsibilities on both parties. These include (but are not limited to) requiring a landlord to:

- Comply with any duties imposed by local laws
- Keep common areas clean and safe
- Keep the premises up to building code
- Maintain appliances furnished with the rental unit
- Maintain the roof, walls, and other structural components
- Provide adequate locks

- Provide pest control
- Supply heat, electricity, and hot and cold water

For tenants, state law requirements include (but are not limited to):

- Comply with the rental agreement
- Dispose of rubbish
- Keep the premises clean
- Not to damage or permit damage to the unit
- Payment of agreed rent
- Properly use fixtures and appliances
- Restore the property to its initial, move-in condition, except for normal wear and tear at the end of the rental

#161.   What local municipality laws must I know?

Local laws vary greatly. Some municipalities have enacted no laws relating to landlord and tenants, while others may have enacted extensive ordinances that include building codes, rent control, zoning, and the licensing of landlord operations.

Local laws may be at the county, city, town, township, or borough level. It is impossible to determine what local laws are without checking with the local municipality.

It is not uncommon for local ordinances to be in force that include trash removal, sidewalk maintenance (especially during severe weather), and the licensure of landlords, including the reporting of current tenants in a rental property. Failing to comply with any local ordinance can result in fines or arrest. It is also common for the local authorities to be enthusiastic in their enforcement of their ordinances and rules about landlording. Perhaps because they are in the community, local government officials often pursue landlords that violate any local rule or ordinance.

#162. **Are there any local health codes that I need to know?**

Many jurisdictions have enacted health codes. These laws can be enacted and enforced by local, county, or state governments. It varies from location, but generally, health codes and laws are common sense. They require a landlord to provide basic services, such as working plumbing for clean drinking water and sanitary sewerage, pest control, and trash removal.

Failing to provide such basic services is unethical, immoral, and usually against the law. Repeated violations of local health codes often label the property owner as a slumlord. Properties that remain in violation of local health codes are typically declared "condemned," and it then becomes unlawful for anyone to live in the building until all code violations are addressed and remedied.

A tenant has a right to expect the landlord to supply a safe and sanitary home. Tenants have the right to call a health or housing inspector if they think there is a code violation in the property they are renting.

#163. **How do I keep up with the changes in laws and regulations?**

Laws that affect landlords change at all levels of government. Whether it is a federal, state, or local law or regulation, there always seems to be another new requirement placed on landlords. Trying to keep up and comply with changes becomes mind-boggling.

Many successful landlords use various sources of information to learn about recent changes in laws that affect them and their rental property ownership. Many rely on their experienced real estate attorneys that send newsletters or other information when laws are changed.

Many also join their local landlord or property management association. Most areas have some kind of local organization that meets regularly (usually for dinner). The latest news about law changes are announced at these meetings. Some larger landlord associations publish newsletters and provide insight into new laws or regulations. Others actively participate in the political process, and oppose or support legislation that will affect their members' operations.

Another source of information for landlords is state associations. By joining, the landlord receives information regularly about changes in laws that affect their rental property.

#164.   What is rent control?

Rent controls are state laws or municipal ordinances that limit the price landlords may charge when renting residential housing. It functions primarily as a price ceiling. Rent control is prevalent in cities with large tenant populations, but it is not uncommon in smaller communities.

Rent control laws are commonly adopted for tenants living in mobile home parks. Reasons given for these rent control laws include residents owning their homes (and renting the land), the high cost of moving "mobile" homes, and the loss of home value when they are moved. However, rent control has expanded to rental units in buildings.

Rent control laws vary among the jurisdictions. Landlords usually have an opportunity to demonstrate that they are not receiving a fair return on their real estate investment. Landlords can prove a rent increase is justified by proving an increase in costs that should be passed on to tenants. Tenants are often able to claim that decreased services or the need of necessary repairs offset rent increases or may justify a rent reduction.

#165.   What is a Section 8 rental?

The Section 8 Rental Voucher Program increases affordable housing choices for very low-income households. A program authorized by the U.S. Department of Housing and Urban Development (HUD), it allows families to choose privately owned rental housing. The local public housing authority (PHA) generally pays the landlord the difference between 30 percent of household income and the PHA-determined payment standard—about 80 to 100 percent of the fair market rent (FMR). The low-income household may choose a unit with a higher rent than the FMR and pay the landlord the difference or choose a lower cost unit and keep the difference.

Through the Section 8 Rental Voucher Program, the local administering housing authority issues a voucher to an income-qualified household, which then finds a unit to rent.

#166. Is seeking a Section 8 tenant a good strategy?

Landlords are assured most of the rental payment each month by the local Public Housing Authority (PHA). Since the landlord knows the rent (or at least most of it) will be paid each month, renting to a Section 8 client is often a smart business strategy.

Many landlords opt not to have a Section 8 client. They wrongly think that only the worse of society are Section 8 clients. Section 8 clients could be single mothers or seniors with only social security income. Many Section 8 clients will live quietly and happily in the property.

Landlords are allowed to select their Section 8 tenants, just as they are with a non-Section 8 client. They can still have an approval process (and they should). The tenant can use the Section 8 payment as part of their income to qualify as a tenant.

Section 8 clients of the local PHA can be the best of tenants. They still need to be screened, and you should reject any applicant that cannot meet the nondiscriminatory guidelines of tenancy.

#167. Are there advantages to having a Section 8 rental property?

There are several benefits and advantages of having your rental property approved as a Section 8 unit. Often the mere certification of the property increases the value. More potential tenants can rent the property. And the property has passed a basic inspection and is certified as being safe and habitable, meeting HUD's rental housing standards.

To other real estate investors, a property that has already been approved by the local Public Housing Authority (PHA) is often more valuable. Real estate investors know that regular rent payments from the PHA are certain. Clients using Section 8 housing often pay their rent without fail, as they do not want to lose the monthly assistance they receive.

Section 8 housing that can be easily modified to accommodate disabled or special needs clients are more valuable. Because of the shortage of these types of rental units, most PHA's authorize a higher monthly rent payment.

#168. **Is it legal to rent a property with black mold?**

Probably not. It is considered a health problem, and it could make the landlord liable for any illness or sickness of the tenant or the tenant's guests.

Molds are fungi. Molds grow throughout the natural and built environment. Tiny particles of mold are present in indoor and outdoor air. In nature, molds help break down dead materials and can be found growing on soil, foods, plant matter, and other items. Molds produce microscopic cells called "spores" which are very tiny and spread easily through the air. Live spores act like seeds, forming new mold growths (colonies) when they find the right conditions.

It is always best when the occupants and building owners work cooperatively to investigate and remove excessive moisture and mold. A common mistake is to "treat" the mold with some chemical (often bleach) or cover it up instead of removing it. Removal of the mold is critical because treated or dead mold can still cause serious health problems.

#169.   **If a tenant claims a property has mold, can they break the lease?**

Probably they can, and do so successfully. It depends on local laws and what, if anything, the landlord does in response to the tenant's complaints.

If the tenant simply vacates the premises and later claims the reason he or she left was that there was mold, they have a weak case. However, if they notified the landlord about the mold and the landlord ignored the problem, there is a strong likelihood they will win any court case. This is especially true if there were multiple notifications to the landlord, and the mold problem was not corrected. If local health codes require mold abatement and the landlord failed to comply, it makes the tenant's likelihood of prevailing stronger.

The tenant, just as the landlord, must be able to prove their side of the case. If the tenant can produce photographs of black mold, copies of letters notifying the landlord of the problem, and medical evidence of sickness, the landlord is likely to lose any claim of monetary loss when the tenant moved out, breaking the lease.

#170.   **If a fire or some other disaster makes the unit uninhabitable, what are my responsibilities to the tenant?**

Most lease agreements include language as to what happens if a fire occurs and makes the property uninhabitable. A rental unit does not need to be totally damaged or destroyed to be uninhabitable. If the unit no longer has a working and usable kitchen, the premises is likely uninhabitable.

It is not uncommon for local authorities to declare the premises uninhabitable after a fire. A building inspector or fire chief might issue a declaration. When that occurs, the lease is terminated.

Renters' insurance provides coverage for additional living expenses for the tenant when the rental unit is damaged by fire or other covered peril. Some landlord property insurance policies may also provide additional living expense coverage to the tenants.

Document the damage to the rental with photographs. Assist the tenant in removing any remaining personal property from the damaged premises. File your property damage claim with your insurance company.

#171. Can a landlord be held responsible for crime against a tenant?

It is possible that a landlord could be successfully sued by a tenant. This is especially true if the landlord did not provide adequate locks for the doors and windows.

Landlords are generally required to take only minimal precautions to protect against foreseeable criminal harm. For example, tenants who are victims of crimes in their building or apartment and who are able to prove that the criminal was an intruder that took advantage of the fact that the entrance to the building was negligently maintained by the landlord, may be able to recover their damages from the landlord. They can successfully bring a costly lawsuit against the landlord, and most likely prevail in the court action.

Don't take basic security lightly. Install lighting in the common areas. Make sure all locks are working properly. Don't put off repairing locks, doorjambs, or installing security locks in the rental property.

#172. What can I legally require of my tenant?

It is reasonable and prudent to expect a tenant to comply with the terms and conditions of the rental agreement or lease. When a tenant deliberately or negligently fails to comply, the landlord has every right to enforce the provisions of the lease agreement.

The landlord should expect (and demand) that the rental unit not be damaged. The tenant and the tenant's guests should not do anything that would destroy or damage the landlord's property.

The tenant should maintain the unit, keeping it clean from debris, trash, and rubbish. The tenant should not do anything that would allow the property to become an unhealthy place to live.

The landlord should rightly expect the tenant to comply with all the rules of the rental that are designed to make the property a safe and pleasant place for people to reside.

To avoid misunderstandings, everything should be placed in writing. Rules should be included as part of the lease agreement.

#173. How can a landlord protect his properties from criminals?

There is probably no single way for a landlord to protect their properties against criminals or criminal acts. However, many little steps might help.

The first step is to approve only good tenants. People with steady employment and reasonable credit are likely to comply with the landlord's rules and not tolerate criminal activity.

Landlords should take steps to eliminate criminal acts. This might include installing security measures, such as dusk-to-dawn lighting, new locks, or repairing fences. In multifamily units, it might mean the installation of security cameras, peepholes in doors, or deadbolt locks.

Landlords should institute and enforce a zero-tolerance criminal activity policy. If a tenant breaks the law in any way, they should be asked to leave. For example, if a tenant is found to possess illegal drugs, do not tolerate it. If they do not voluntarily leave, commence eviction proceeding.

#174. Can a landlord require the tenant to sign written agreements?

A rule can most likely be established that requires the tenant to accept communications from the landlord. The purpose is to acknowledge receipt of the communication, but not that the tenant agrees with the content.

A letter that the landlord sends to the tenant warning about a rule violation could include a statement that says something like, "I acknowledge receipt of this correspondence" with a signature block and date. The landlord can request the acknowledgement be signed and returned by the tenant. If sent via the mail, include a self-addressed, stamped envelope for the tenant's use in returning the copy to you.

The landlord can (and should) refuse to initiate the rental unless a lease agreement is signed by the tenant. Other documents, such as rules of the premises, should also be signed by the tenant. The landlord should always provide copies of any documents signed by the tenant to the tenant for their records.

#175. What can I do if a tenant wants to break the lease and move?

You can agree to the termination of the lease or not. The tenant may have a legitimate reason for leaving, such as a change in employment status. Contrary to the popular belief of most tenants, there are no provisions in law that permit tenants to break a lease if they buy a house or get a job transfer.

Tenants who need to move out early have three options:

- Negotiating with the landlord to end the lease early
- Breaking the lease
- Subletting

All tenants may break their leases, even if the landlord says that subletting is the only option. When a tenant wants to move, it may be possible to negotiate a suitable agreement.

The lease agreement may include provisions as to how an early termination of the lease can occur. There may be a provision that allows for early termination with the payment of a fee.

#176. **Why should I allow a tenant to break a lease?**

There are several reasons why a landlord may allow a tenant to break a lease. They include:

- You want to avoid a dispute with your tenant
- You desire to avoid court costs of the collection or eviction process
- The tenant offers or agrees to pay an early termination fee
- You would like to do work on the apartment
- You could rent the unit for more than its current rate

You may be willing to sign an early termination to the lease because it makes the most sense to do so. There is not much a landlord can do once a tenant has decided to move from the rental unit. It doesn't matter what the language of the lease agreement says. It is often best to negotiate with the tenant.

Getting the tenant out without damaging the unit and properly terminating the rental agreement so the landlord can rent the unit to someone else often makes sense. Successful landlords often work with the tenant to terminate a lease early.

#177. **What is mitigation?**

In some areas, the landlord may be required legally to mitigate (or lessen) the loss of rental income when a tenant moves out and breaks the lease agreement. For example, suppose the tenant moves out, and still owes six months of rent at $1,000 per month. The landlord may want the $6,000 from the tenant, but the courts may not grant that amount in a judgment to the landlord. Many courts have ruled that the landlord has the obligation to mitigate the damages by trying to find a new tenant.

To prove the landlord has attempted to mitigate the loss, the landlord must:

- Advertise the rental unit
- Show the rental property to interested applicants

The landlord may charge the actual costs associated with re-renting a rental unit, but not for the time spent. The landlord may not steer any applicant to a unit that has been vacated by someone breaking a lease.

#178. **Is the landlord ever permitted to break a lease?**

Generally, no. A landlord is not permitted to break a lease. A landlord cannot increase the rent or change the terms of the rental agreement if there is a valid written lease in effect.

If a landlord wants a tenant out of the premises (assuming the tenant has done nothing wrong and has not violated any of the terms of the lease or rental rules), the landlord can negotiate with the tenant to move. Both the landlord and the tenant would need to agree to the lease termination, which should be placed in writing.

To get a tenant to move under these circumstances, it usually takes money. By the landlord paying the tenant, a negotiated termination is often achieved. It may take the payment of one or two months' rent to get the tenant to move.

Landlords should not try to evict a tenant without cause. Remember that the tenant has the right of a hearing, and the landlord will have to explain to a judge why he is evicting a tenant. As long as the tenant has not violated any of the lease terms, the eviction order will not be issued.

#179.   How does a landlord legally evict a tenant?

Eviction is a legal process. The procedure to evict varies among localities. The landlord seeks a court order for the tenant to leave the property (with all their personal property). If the tenant refuses to obey the court order, the court will use officers of the court (constables, sheriffs, etc.) to remove the individuals from the premises.

Often, when an eviction is sought by the landlord, there is also a claim for money included. This could be for unpaid rent or damages.

The first step should be to ask the tenant to leave the premises voluntarily. Try to resolve the move without going to court. It is cheaper and faster, in most circumstances. Some successful landlords have actually helped problem tenants to move by offering a free rental truck or a refund of a portion of rent if they agree to move by a specific date.

#180.   If there is no written lease, how do I initiate an eviction?

All jurisdictions have established rules as to how an eviction must proceed. The action is always started by the landlord and is against the tenant. In most cases, this is considered a landlord/tenant dispute and is usually heard in a small claims court. Although the court may not be as formal as higher courts, rules must be strictly followed by both sides.

Landlords often claim damages or money is owed during an eviction proceeding. Tenants are often permitted to file a counterclaim against the landlord.

When the case is scheduled for court, the case is usually heard at the predetermined date and time. Seldom will a small claims court continue a landlord/tenant case to a later date.

Both sides will be given an opportunity to explain their side to the judge. The judge typically makes an immediate decision. If the judge grants the eviction, the tenant is ordered to vacate the premises. If the tenant fails to do so, the landlord must return to court and seek the court's assistance in enforcing the order.

#181.   **What rights does the tenant have if a landlord refuses to make repairs?**

It depends on several factors. It depends on what type of repairs are needed, and whether the tenant or landlord is being unreasonable.

If it is an emergency repair, a court will always rule in favor of the tenant. For example, if a pipe is leaking and the landlord refuses to repair it, the court is likely to rule it was reasonable for the tenant to call a plumber and seek reimbursement for the cost of the repair.

If it is a nonemergency situation, such as a dishwasher not working, it's a matter of what is reasonable or not. If the dishwasher was included as part of the rental and the tenant informed the landlord that the dishwasher needs repairs, then after a reasonable time, it should be fixed or replaced.

A tenant would have the right to request reimbursement for necessary repairs. If the landlord refuses to pay for the damages, the tenant could file an action in a small claims court to recover their money.

#182.   **When can a tenant sublet a rental unit?**

Subletting a rental unit is permitted only when this provision is included in the lease agreement. When a tenant sublets a rental unit, they are still on the lease and responsible for the rent payments, even though the tenant will no longer be living in the rental unit.

If the person the tenant sublets to does not pay the rent or damages the rental unit, the tenant remains financially responsible. Subletting can be risky to the tenant. When permitted by a lease agreement to sublet, the tenant may want to invoke the provision and sublet to a friend or relative. This is done when the tenant plans to return to the same rental unit after a time away.

Tenants with year-to-year leases usually can sublet without the landlord's permission, unless the lease says otherwise. Many landlords will not sign a lease without this type of provision. The reasons are simple: the landlord wants to approve those living in his rental property. In addition, the landlord does not want to deal with a tenant that is no longer living in the immediate area.

#183. **What can a landlord do when a tenant sublets a property without permission to do so?**

When the landlord learns the property has been sublet, an immediate decision needs to be made. The landlord should either accept or deny the sublet. Of course, the first step is to check to make sure a sublet is permitted or prohibited in the lease agreement.

If the sublet is prohibited, the landlord should immediately inform the tenant and move toward an eviction of the person in the premises. If the tenant and landlord agree to a termination of the lease and the new tenant applies and seeks approval to rent the premises, it could be just a matter of drawing up a new rental agreement. The landlord may want to charge a fee for this service or waive any fees associated.

If the person subletting is not approved by the landlord, then eviction should be immediately commenced.

#184. **Can a landlord evict a tenant for selling drugs or gang activity?**

Yes. No community will have sympathy for a tenant actively engaged in the sale of illegal drugs or violent gang activity. However, the landlord always needs to prove the case before a judge in small claims court when an eviction order is sought.

Proving a tenant is selling drugs or involved in gang activity might be a problem. Obviously, if the tenant has been arrested by the police and is in jail awaiting trial, the landlord's position is going to be easier to prove.

Mere suspicion of illegal activity will not be enough to get an eviction order. Since you must be able to prove your case, begin by observing the activity at your premises. Keep careful records. Gather photographic evidence, if possible. Seek the assistance of neighbors, other tenants, or local authorities.

Enforce a zero-tolerance for illegal activity. In a civil action, such as an eviction, you do not have to prove your case "beyond a reasonable doubt" but only by a "preponderance of the evidence."

#185. **Is a landlord permitted to evict a tenant during the winter?**

Unless there is a local law prohibiting the eviction, a tenant can be evicted during the winter months. Although it is unlikely that an eviction (the physical removal of a person or property) will occur a few days before Christmas, the courts usually have the authority to order an eviction despite the time of the year.

Some tenants have confused evictions with a "no-shut-off" rule that many jurisdictions have put into place. This rule prevents utilities from shutting off service during the winter months. After reports of people dying from no heat, public utility commissions adopted rules that heat or other utilities cannot be turned off for nonpayment during the winter months. Some people think wrongly that this also applies to landlords and the payment of rent, but it does not.

#186. **Does a tenant that is elderly, disabled, or pregnant have any special rights?**

Generally, no. When a tenant is being evicted for just cause, the judge will not give extra legal weight to the tenant because of their condition. Judges are human and might feel some compassion toward the tenant. The judge may be a bit more lenient or understanding, and try to find a fair resolution.

Tenants that are pregnant or disabled are persons that evoke sympathy. It may be best for the landlord to try to work out a compromise, if possible. Sometimes, local charities, welfare agencies, or churches may be a source of income for these tenants. Directing them toward such resources may get the rent paid and avoid an immediate eviction. By doing so, the landlord might resolve the immediate problem. It would also show the judge that the landlord has tried to get help for the tenant.

If possible, it is best to try to avoid confrontations in court. However, that doesn't mean you cannot win just because the tenant has an obvious physical condition.

#187. **How can a landlord avoid the eviction process?**

Avoiding the eviction process often makes sense to the landlord. Work to resolve tenant disputes. Most can be resolved quickly and quietly. If you become angered with your tenant, walk away. Do not do anything rash or precipitous. Take some time before deciding what to do.

Many times, the disputes are minor and only escalate because of personality conflicts. Tenants aren't always going to do what you want. They may do exactly what you do not want.

If you tell them no pets, some tenants will get one and hide it from you. For example, they will get a cat. They try to dispose of the kitty litter. They pour it down the toilet, only to hide the fact they have a cat from you. How you learn about all of this is when you receive a $195 repair bill from the plumber. Give yourself a cool down period before confronting the tenant.

#188. Should a landlord ever be lenient with a late-paying tenant?

No. Establishing a prudent collection policy saves hours of agonizing decision making later. Having a policy already in place saves you from having to decide something like, "Should I really evict poor old widow Smith?"

Your policy should follow guidelines similar to the following: Rent should be due on the first of the month. There is a grace period of up to five days. During this time, payment can still be made without incurring a late fee. After the fifth day, a reminder notice can be distributed and a late fee of $10 per day applies.

On the eighth day of the month, a quit or pay (or equivalent legal notice) notice is served upon the tenant. By the fifteenth of the month, file the eviction notice in court on any unpaid tenants.

The goal is to never allow a tenant to get more than thirty days behind in rent.

#189. How long does a landlord have to start a court action against a tenant?

The amount of time the landlord has to commence court actions vary from state to state. All jurisdictions will have some kind of statute of limitations. This is the maximum amount of time anyone has to start a legal action.

There is no grace period. If the law states the statute of limitations is 180 days, you will not be able to commence an action 181 days later. In some jurisdictions, you may get an extra day only if the last day falls on a Sunday or legal holiday. Of course, this provision will be clearly stated in the law.

Most courts (and their clerks) will not accept a complaint or action from you if your action is not commenced within the statute of limitations. If the action is started, and the tenant can prove it was not filed within the proper period, the judge will dismiss the landlord's complaint.

#190. How long does a tenant have to start a court action against the landlord?

Just as the landlord is limited in starting a court action after a specific date, so is the tenant. The theory of law is simple: someone should not have to defend himself or herself years later.

Each jurisdiction has established the statute of limitations for such court actions. Some are set at only a few months, while others will have longer periods, such as one or two years. It is for this reason that landlords should maintain their entire rental records for several years after a tenant vacates a property.

Tenants may have happily moved, but sometime later, perhaps while at a party or some other social event, overhear someone bragging about successfully suing and collecting money from a former landlord. Suddenly, as a past landlord, you have become a target.

The statute of limitations can help the landlord. If the action was started too late, the landlord can seek a dismissal of the complaint from the court. It is an absolute defense, and the judge should rule in favor of the landlord when the action was started after the statute of limitations.

#191.   **Should a landlord avoid small claims court?**

Yes and no. The landlord should not be afraid of going to small claims court, either as a plaintiff or a defendant. Appearing in court is, unfortunately, a part of the landlord business.

Landlords do not need an attorney when appearing in small claims court. For the most part, they can handle their own case. As long as they are properly prepared and are reasonable, they can win. When a landlord loses a case, the small claims court's decision can usually be appealed to a higher court. At that level, it is usually best to engage the services of an attorney.

Avoiding court, whenever possible, is often a wise business decision. If a settlement can be reached before court, both sides usually win. There is nothing certain when going to court. Even if a landlord wins, that is no guarantee payment or vacancy will occur quickly. If a tenant is willing to move or offers some payment, consider the proposal.

#192.   **Is a landlord responsible for a defective appliance?**

If the appliance is part of the rental agreement, the landlord is responsible for maintenance, repair, or replacement of the appliance.

Some appliances are essential to the rental unit. For example, a working refrigerator or a range/oven is needed to make the unit habitable. If the landlord provided these appliances as a condition of the rental, then their maintenance is required.

As a landlord, put yourself in the tenant's position. The tenant cannot be expected to live in a rental unit without a working refrigerator. Food is expensive. The tenant needs a refrigerator. While it may not make you happy to have to repair or purchase a refrigerator, it is necessary to do so. Repair appliances quickly for the tenant.

#193. **What is a rent escalator clause?**

This is a provision placed in a lease agreement. It is a section of the rental agreement that calls for an increase in the monthly rent. The increase is usually set to take place at a certain time and is often indicated by a specific amount or percentage. For example, the rent escalation provision might state that the rent will increase $25 per month on July 1, or by 5 percent after the first twelve months.

Sometimes rent escalation clauses are written to increase the rental costs in the event of an increase in certain costs, such as utilities. For example, an escalator clause may specify that rent due will increase with inflation.

A rental escalation clause is the opposite of the de-escalation clause. These are seldom, if ever, used in a residential rental agreement.

#194. **When should a landlord call the police about a tenant?**

The landlord should always report any illegal or criminal activity to the police. It doesn't matter if the tenant is suspected of wrong-doing or not.

Do not tolerate criminal activity on your rental property. Be quick to complain and report unlawful acts to your local authorities. Assist the local law enforcement agency by being a good citizen and an excellent witness.

Participate in and cooperate with any anti-crime programs. Encourage your tenants to do the same. No one wants to live among crooks, thieves, or thugs. As the landlord, do your part to eliminate such activity.

Remember too that a landlord could (and likely will) be held legally liable for allowing criminal activity on their premises, especially if someone is injured or assaulted. It is not uncommon for a victim to make a personal injury claim against the property owner. Your best defense is to show that you have reported all known illegal activity to the proper local law enforcement authorities.

#195. Can a landlord pester a tenant until they leave the property?

Harassment in any form is illegal. A landlord cannot harass a tenant into vacating a rental property.

Naïve or inexperienced landlords are under the misconception that harassment tactics can work. The removal of locks, doors, or windows has been unsuccessfully tried in the past. Turning off heat, water, or utilities is another foolhardy method that will just be viewed as harassment by a court.

Withholding of services such as trash removal, making verbal threats, making loud noises during quiet times, or any other form of harassment by the landlord could cause the filing of criminal or civil charges. In some jurisdictions, landlord harassment carries harsh penalties.

Landlord harassment is usually defined as the willing creation of conditions that are uncomfortable for the tenants. It is done in order to induce the abandonment of a rental contract. Such a strategy, although illegal, is often commenced because it avoids costly legal expenses and potential problems with eviction.

#196. Should I accept the rent after I file an eviction notice with the court?

Yes. At any time, you can accept the back rent, late fees (if any), and the court costs from the tenant. After receiving payment, the court action seeking eviction can be dismissed.

Do not accept a partial payment and drop the legal action. Keep the pressure on the tenant by proceeding with the eviction order. Until all amounts are paid in full, don't stop the eviction action.

If the landlord is evicting for nonpayment of rent, accepting partial rent from tenants after the eviction process is commenced shouldn't jeopardize the eviction case. The legal issue is whether accepting rent waives the landlord's right to evict the tenant. Waiver can be a matter of intent. The question is: Did someone, by taking a certain action, intend to give up a right they had?

Landlords who accept rent in the middle of the eviction process rarely intend to forfeit their right to evict their tenant. Landlords simply want to minimize their losses by collecting as much as they can and not waive any of their legal rights.

#197. **Can I proceed with eviction even if the rent is paid by the tenant?**

Probably not.

If the eviction was started based solely on unpaid rent and the rent was paid, the case before the small claims court is no longer valid. If you want to evict the tenant, even when the rent is paid, then you probably will need to start another eviction action. Of course, you will need grounds or a legitimate reason to evict. Just because the rent was paid late but was paid after collection efforts on the landlord's part is not likely to persuade a judge to issue an eviction notice.

Don't take retaliatory actions against the tenant. If a tenant exercises rights under the law, such as bringing their account current, complaining to a government authority, or deducting for repairs as provided by statute, the law prohibits the landlord from taking retaliatory action. Examples of retaliatory actions are raising the rent, reducing services, or evicting the tenant.

If the matter is taken to court and the judge finds in favor of the tenant, the landlord can be ordered to reverse his or her actions, as well as pay for any harm done to the tenant, and possibly pay the tenant's attorney fees.

#198.   What should I do when the tenant vacates the property?

Tenants move out of the rental property either in a friendly or combative manner. Hopefully, the landlord can keep the move-out and turnover a friendly and happy experience. Ideally, after the tenant has emptied the rental unit, removing all clothing, furniture, personal property, and completed a general cleaning, a time can be arranged for a walk through inspection. Both the tenant and the landlord inspect the property jointly, and both agree to any damage found. The keys to the rental unit are turned over by the tenant, and the rental has been completed. Within the next few days, the security deposit is returned to the tenant.

It is best to try to conclude the rental amicably and without hostility. The goal should be to get the tenant out, get their account closed, and find a new tenant as quickly as possible.

#199.   What kind of inspection should I do when the property is vacated?

A complete property inspection should be completed of your rental unit as soon as possible after the unit has been vacated. It should not be delayed for any reason. You want to make sure the unit is safe and nothing has been done that could cause damage or expense, such as the thermostat set high or a faucet allowed to run. For this reason, the inspection should be within twenty-four hours, but the same day may be best.

Using the same form as your move-in report, go through the rental unit and note all damage, debris, and observations. Be sure to document problems by photographing them (use disposable film cameras that can produce images that could prove your assertion in small claims court).

Prepare your report so it is readable and clear. Be prepared to photocopy it so a copy can be delivered to the former tenant.

PART 5

Controlling Expenses

You are in the landlord business to make money. How well you control your expenses will often make the difference between your landlord business being profitable or not. This section of the book covers how to operate the business profitably by watching and controlling your expenses. It will give you ideas and suggestions that could save you thousands of dollars and put that money where it belongs: in your pocket.

#200. Should I pay for trash removal?

It is common for the landlord to pay for trash removal service. If the rental property is a single-family residence, often the trash service is then paid by the tenant, but not always.

In multifamily rental properties, the landlord customarily pays for the trash removal service. This expense is covered as part of the monthly rent.

Excessive trash or waste is often more expensive to haul away. Special items, such as furniture, often incur an additional charge by the trash hauler. While it is desirable to have the tenant pay for these additional charges, it is not always easy to get a tenant to do so.

Tenants can leave behind an inordinate amount of trash when they vacate a rental unit. Broken furniture, clothing, books, boxes of household goods, and garbage are often abandoned.

When an arrangement is made for the tenant to pay for trash removal, it is always best to bill the tenant for the service and monitor the payment. Allowing the tenant to pay the trash hauler directly can result in no service because of unpaid bills.

#201. How can I be sure the tenant pays for the trash, gas, water, or sewer bills?

The easiest way to make sure the bill is paid is to have the bill mailed to the landlord, and then the landlord bills the tenant. Demand payment within ten to fourteen days. Tenants can (and will) forget to pay some bills.

One easy way to make sure the bills are always paid is to include the estimated bill in the actual rental. If the water bill is $20 per month, simply add that to the monthly payment before renting the unit.

Some landlords, however, find it advantageous to offer a lower monthly rent, and ask the tenant to pay the bill when received. This allows the landlord to quote a smaller rental payment and makes the tenant pay for the service actually used.

To make sure the tenant pays the bill, the landlord needs to receive the payment from the tenant, and then pay the bill directly.

#202. **What kinds of insurance do I need?**

You must purchase the right insurance to protect you against losses. Insurance is simply the transfer of risk to another. People buy insurance to transfer the risk of loss to insurance. In the event of a loss, the insurer reimburses the loss of the insured, in accordance with the terms and conditions of the insurance policy.

As a landlord, you need to protect your property against losses from accidental occurrences, such as fires, severe weather, or automobile collisions. You must also protect yourself against claims or a lawsuit that allege negligence that caused bodily injury or property damage to someone else.

Insurance never protects you against deliberate acts. Insurance only covers you against accidental or unintended acts. If you deliberately assaulted a tenant, insurance would not protect you against criminal charges filed against you.

#203. **What is tenant relocation insurance?**

Tenant relocation insurance pays for the moving expenses associated with finding and moving to a new living space when their current rental unit has become inhabitable because of fire or other accidental loss. In some locales, this insurance must be purchased by the landlord and be available to the tenant after a loss. In other areas, the tenant is responsible for purchasing this coverage, which is a part of the renter's insurance policy.

Tenant relocation insurance provides specific coverage. It will provide reimbursement costs for moving expenses, storage, and packing personal property. It often covers the cost of searching for replacement housing. It does not provide reimbursement for deposits or security payments.

The coverage often has a limit or maximum payout. The maximum amount of coverage is usually for the rental unit and not per tenant. There is no deductible for claims filed for tenant relocation insurance.

#204. **What is rent loss insurance?**

Rent loss insurance is what it sounds like. You pay a premium not just to cover any loss to the house but also if you lose rent. In some policies, not having a tenant is enough to trigger a claim payment to you. Some policies will pay the landlord a predetermined amount of money should a rental unit not produce rent. When you cannot collect rent payments because a catastrophic event makes the unit uninhabitable until repaired, you receive a monthly payment from the insurer until your property is repaired. The amount you receive and how long you can collect payments depends on your coverage.

Rent loss insurance typically provides a minimum of six months gross rental income should income stop due to a covered hazard, such as a fire, damage due to a falling tree, or a vehicle striking the building.

Some lending guidelines make rent loss insurance a requirement and not just an option. Recent changes in Freddie Mac (FHLMC) guidelines require that if an operating loss can be expected when acquiring a first investment property, additional rent loss insurance coverage is required for the loan to be approved.

#205. **Do I need flood insurance?**

If your rental property is located within a flood plain, you need flood insurance. If you have or acquire financing, your lender will likely require that you purchase flood insurance to protect their investment in your property.

Flood insurance is available for rental properties that are located in communities that participate in the National Flood Insurance Program (NFIP). The U.S. Congress established the program with the passage of the National Flood Insurance Act of 1968. The NFIP is a federal program enabling property owners in participating communities to purchase insurance as protection against flood losses in exchange for state and community floodplain management regulations that reduce future flood damages.

Often property coverage excludes floor or groundwater damage. Ask your agent if you are protected against the water main breaking for no apparent reason (such as the ground shifting), flooding your property, and causing a wall to cave. Many landlords are not properly protected for this type of peril, yet the damage can be devastating.

#206.   What type of liability insurance do I need?

Liability insurance protects you against legal claims made against you by others because of your negligence. In today's litigious society, liability insurance is not a luxury. It is an absolute necessity. Personal injury attorneys are very adept at developing theories of liability and suing property owners.

The insurance is sold with a maximum amount of coverage that will be paid for any alleged negligence. Common amounts of coverage include $100,000, $300,000, $500,000, or $1 million. Typically, higher amounts (more than $1 million) of liability insurance are sold within what the insurance companies call umbrella insurance.

Most liability insurance includes medical coverage. Although modest in limits, the idea is that even if someone is hurt or injured on your property, even though you are not negligent, the medical bills are covered. For example, if someone stumbles for no reason or defect on the sidewalk but lacerated their hand, the medical coverage would pay for treatment up to a specific amount of the coverage.

#207. **What type of property coverage insurance should I purchase?**

Property insurance protects you against any *accidental* damages that might be occurring to your property. This type of insurance always includes a limit—the maximum amount your policy will pay out for a total loss. A deductible—which is the amount you pay first for the loss—is also included.

Property insurance is often called fire insurance. You can buy a policy that would just protect you from the loss of fire damage, but this is seldom done today. Other perils, such as damage caused by wind, rain, automobile, vandalism, and other accidental and unintended damages, are routinely covered under today's property insurance policies.

If you have a mortgage, the amount of your loan will determine the minimum amount of insurance you must purchase. You should buy enough insurance to replace your building should there be a total loss. Even though the land will still be there, make sure you have enough insurance to cover your losses.

#208. **How much insurance is enough?**

There is no specific guideline to say exactly how much insurance is enough to cover any possible loss. This is particularly true of liability insurance. What it takes to protect you against any possible lawsuit is difficult to determine.

With property coverage, it is easier to ascertain the maximum amount of your potential loss. If the building were to be destroyed, you could cover your loss by having the building rebuilt (replacement cost) or by being paid what you have invested in the property (reimbursement). It is easy to determine these amounts.

But the uncertainty of litigation and lawsuits makes it much more difficult to determine how much your legal liability exposure might be. You should discuss this with both your insurance professional and your attorney. Most likely, your insurance professional will recommend the purchase of an umbrella policy, which will provide additional liability insurance coverage. Your attorney may suggest additional or different insurance coverage, or the formation of a corporation to protect your assets.

#209. What kind of financing should I seek for rental property purchases?

For rental income property, you need non-owner-occupied (NOO) financing programs. Some lenders will not be interested in lending money for NOO purchases or refinancing. Others will have developed special programs and actively seek your business.

You should seek financing that simply makes sense. You usually want the lowest interest rate, the longest possible financing term, and the lowest costs to originate the loan.

The monthly payment is always important. You do not want to create a negative cash flow. For example, if your monthly payment is $1,000, but the maximum rent you can realistically collect is $800, then you have created monthly negative cash flow of $200. Your financing should allow you to have a positive cash flow. You need to borrow less by making a larger down payment.

The amount of the monthly payment will be determined by how many payments are to be made (most landlords seek thirty year— 360 months—financing).

#210. Should I ever pay financing points?

Paying points—either an "origination fee" or a "discount" fee— should be carefully weighed with all offers of financing. Origination fees are often 1 percent of the total amount of the loan. The discount fee is used to buy down an interest rate. For example, a lender might offer a 6.5 percent interest rate on a loan, or a 6 percent interest rate with the payment of 1 percent discount fee. A point is always the equivalent of 1 percent. Two points would be 2 percent of the amount being borrowed from the lender.

It does sometimes make sense to pay points, as long as you are going to remain in the property and keep the financing in place. Often it requires two to four years before paying points makes financial sense. However, you never know until you sit down and calculate different offers and options available to you. Once your loan application is approved, the lender is likely to offer different financing options to you—some with and some without the payment of points. If you are going to sell the property within the next few years, paying points will not likely make sense.

#211. **Is it better to use a bank or a mortgage company for rental property financing?**

For the most part, it doesn't matter whether your loan is originated by a bank or a mortgage company. It is unlikely that the loan will remain with the bank or mortgage company. Most will sell the loan, transferring it to another entity. Some do this instantly, while others do it later, after acquiring other loans and bundling them into a package. When this happens, the terms (interest rate, payments, etc.) cannot be changed on you.

As a real estate investor and landlord, you are looking for the best possible terms for your loan. In other words, you want the best deal. You are looking for the loan that costs you the least amount of money. It doesn't matter if that deal comes from a bank or a mortgage company.

A local bank may be a better option for an unusual property. A property with more than four rental units or a property that might be considered commercial (a store/retail space on the first floor, with apartments on the upper floors) might be more appealing to a community bank than another, out-of-the-area lender.

#212. **What are some ways to pay less for financing?**

Shopping for financing is probably the single best way to pay less. Banks and mortgage companies can become extremely competitive when they need to be. They will reduce interest rates and closing costs to snag financing they want in their portfolio.

Several factors determine financing costs. They are:

- Your credit rating
- Loan-to-value (LTV)
- Type of property
- Ability to pay back the loan

The higher your credit rating, the better rates you will be offered. The lower the LTV, the better the rate (if you want an 80 percent LTV loan, you are likely to get a better financing deal than a loan with a 95 percent LTV).

The type of property often determines the financing deal, too. The condition of the property can be a factor. The property is the collateral; the lender is investing in that real estate. The better shape it is in, the better.

The lender will also determine your ability to make the monthly mortgage payments. The more positive cash flow you can show from the property, the better financing package you will be offered.

#213. **When should I refinance my rental property?**

Everyone knows they should refinance their debt when they can to obtain a lower interest rate. If you are paying 8 percent interest, and you can move the debt to a 6 percent rate, of course you refinance. That only makes sense.

On a $200,000, thirty year loan, the difference of a monthly payment between an 8 percent and 6 percent rate is substantial. The 6 percent payment is $1,199.10 and the 8 percent payment is $1,467.53, a difference of $268.43 per month. There is no logical reason not to refinance.

You don't have to wait until the mortgage interest rate drops by 2 percent before you consider refinancing the mortgage on your rental property. The decision to refinance your investment properties is dependent on many things, including:

- How much lower the interest rate is on the new loan
- What the costs are for the new loan
- What your equity position in the property is
- How long you plan to keep your property
- Whether you plan to do a cash-out refinancing

#214. **What should I consider when setting an operating budget?**

Using a simple spreadsheet, identify your ongoing monthly expenses. These include such things as your business telephone line, Internet service, accounting service, etc.

Also, determine what your major expenses are likely to be over the next three years, and plan for them. This does not include real estate you will acquire, but rather items of $500 or more that you need for your business. In a three-year period, you will probably experience at least one hardware and software computer upgrade.

Developing an operating budget is tricky. Most beginners may underestimate the costs of running their own office. Entire expense categories can be omitted. For instance, you should probably budget something for continuing education, seminars, or conferences. What about the travel expenses to attend these conferences? Then there are professional dues, extra phone lines, perhaps a cell phone for emergencies, auto expenses, office supplies, subscription services, and more.

#215. What is the life expectancy of appliances?

Various appliances have different life expectancies. According to the National Association of Home Builders, of the major appliances in a home, gas ranges have the longest life expectancy: fifteen years. Dryers and refrigerators last about thirteen years. Some of the appliances with the shortest lifespan are compactors (six years), dishwashers (nine years), and microwave ovens (nine years). Washing machines last about eleven years. Single door refrigerators seem to last longer than other styles.

The life expectancy of a typical appliance depends largely on the use it receives. Heavily used appliances need to be replaced sooner than those used less. Many times, many consumers replace appliances long before they are worn out because changes in styling, technology, and consumer preferences make newer products more desirable. Landlords usually do not make this kind of replacement. Rather, as long as the appliance is functioning, it is not replaced or updated.

#216. How can I save money on appliances?

Appliances are often problematic for landlords. Not only do they need to be purchased and installed, but also they need to be maintained.

One way to save money on appliances is to allow the tenant to provide them. If the landlord does not provide a washer and dryer but has the hookups for these appliances, it then becomes an option for the tenant to purchase and install them. If the appliance malfunctions, it is up to the tenant to repair their appliance.

Scratched, damaged, or dented appliances (which are usually discounted because of the blemishes) are often attractive purchases to the landlord. They are still quite functional and usually have the same guarantee as units that are not slightly damaged.

Some landlords purchase used appliances for their rental units. They also buy appliances with outdated or less popular colors.

When you purchase new appliances for a rental unit, you can raise the rent to cover the cost. The general guideline is that one-fortieth of the cost of the appliance is the amount the rent should be increased. If a $400 appliance is installed in the rental unit, the rent should be increased $10 per month (1/40 of $400 = $10).

#217. Can I require a tenant to clean the rental unit when he moves?

You can certainly try. Some tenants will leave your unit sparkling clean, while others will leave it filthy. Those that leave the unit dirty often leave behind trash, garbage, and other junk.

Some landlords require a professional carpet cleaning to be paid by the tenant. After the tenant leaves, the landlord schedules the cleaning and it is paid from the security deposit.

To make the cleaning enforceable, it must be part of the lease agreement. Include terms that require the tenant to leave the unit clean and rubbish free.

During your inspection of the unit after your tenant vacates, take photographs of excessively dirty conditions and rubbish. Use one of those throwaway film cameras (so you have the negatives) to show a judge, should the matter end up in court. Remember that you must be able to prove your case. If you say it was dirty and the tenant says it was clean, your showing the judge pictures of the condition of the unit could be the difference between winning and losing your case in court.

#218. What type of maintenance should I routinely schedule?

Each year, you should completely inspect each rental unit you own. This should be done at roughly the same time.

Real estate, unlike other investments, requires you to be actively involved in maintaining it and fixing problems and addressing issues.

Your inspection should include:

- Check the mechanical systems (heating/cooling/electrical/plumbing).
- Check the paint—especially the exterior—for signs of cracking, peeling, and exposed wood.
- Check for cracks in concrete or asphalt.
- Roofs. Make certain the roof is functioning. If there are any leaks or loose shingles, fix them immediately.
- Landscaping often needs to be updated and freshened. Bushes and shrubs need to be trimmed, as do some trees. Mulch is often needed.
- Unsafe conditions.

#219. Should I do my own repairs?

Any repairs you can do yourself will save you money. And every dollar you save on repairs is money in your pocket. If you can eliminate $1,000 in repairs per year, that's $1,000 more that you have made on your rental unit. This doesn't mean you should avoid repairs, but rather if you can take on the little things, you can save substantial expenses.

Some of the minor repairs/maintenance that you can do yourself include:

- Changing air filters in heating/air conditioner units
- Installing batteries in smoke detectors
- Landscaping fixes such as trimming bushes, mulching, and planting
- Painting
- Replacing the parts inside the toilet
- Fixing cabinet doors and drawers
- Replacing light bulbs
- Changing locks
- Clearing clogged drains
- Patching drywall

There are some things beyond the normal handyman scope of repairs or maintenance. There are times when it is best to call in a professional. But for those easier and less complicated tasks, you could make more money from your rental property by doing the work yourself.

#220.   **What repairs are tenants responsible for paying?**

Tenants are generally not responsible for paying for any repairs to the rental unit. One of the advantages of renting is that the renter incurs no expense when something breaks or needs replacing.

Normal wear and tear is to be expected and is not the responsibility of a tenant. If the landlord provides a clothes washer to a tenant, it will someday stop functioning. That's just common sense and predictable. Landlords should not expect a tenant to pay for something that wears out.

Damage is not normal wear and tear. The tenant should pay for all damage. The tenant should pay for the repairs needed because of deliberate or accidental acts. For example, if the tenant spills red wine on the landlord's white carpet, the tenant should pay the expense of removing the stain, or if it cannot be removed, the cost of replacing the carpet.

Dirt is not damage. Some jurisdictions allow landlords to charge for the cleanup of dirt, while others do not. Excessive dirt or filth is allowed in many areas.

#221. How do I maximize my tax deductions?

Current tax laws offer various deductions that landlords may use to minimize the tax liability. Any legitimate tax deduction should be used to maximize the amount you can use to reduce your taxes legally.

Always maintain excellent records. Keep receipts for everything. Maintain a log of miles driven because of your rental property business. You are entitled, for example, to deduct mileage from your home office to the post office to mail notices to the tenant. However, the time, date, and purpose of the trip should be accurately recorded in a log to prove the legitimacy of the mileage expense.

Look for all legal and appropriate deductions. For example, if you maintain a home office for running your business, you can deduct the expenses associated with the office. Although the IRS has repeatedly said that it closely examines such deductions, that is no reason not to deduct the expense. As long as you fully comply with the regulations and can prove your expenses, you should claim the deductions.

#222. What do I need to know about the IRS Schedule E?

The Schedule E is attached to a 1040 annual return. It is used to determine profit (or loss) from Rental Property. Profit from rental properties is treated as income on your tax return.

The key to mastering the Schedule E is to organize your income and expenses using a spreadsheet or personal finance software program. Landlords who keep detailed summaries of their rental property expenses are the ones who benefit most at tax time from the generous tax rules regarding rental income.

Although the Schedule E can become quite complex and involved for larger corporations involved in real estate income property, it is not that difficult to comprehend. The IRS instructions for the form are involved. You should study this form and try to complete it before turning it over to the professional tax preparer. By doing so, the cost of preparing this form can be greatly reduced.

Renting real estate property is generally considered a passive activity by the IRS, even if you devote a substantial amount of time to selecting the tenants, repairing the rental unit, and inspecting the property for routine maintenance. What this really means is that the IRS limits your losses from your rental business to a maximum of $25,000 per year.

#223.   **What amount can I claim as depreciation?**

Depreciation is the loss of value of property from its natural deterioration. A legitimate tax deduction, the IRS has established rules in how this expense relates to the natural deterioration that happens to almost any long-lasting asset.

Most landlords think of the permitted depreciation in terms of buildings. For example, most residential buildings have a depreciation period of twenty-seven and a half years. This means that you can deduct 1/27.5 (3.63636 percent) of the building's value as an expense each year. You can do so until you've owned the building for 27.5 years.

To determine the building's value, multiply the purchase price by this ratio: building assessment divided by the overall assessment (you may not depreciate the value of the land where the building is located).

In most cases, it often makes sense to depreciate items in a building separately from the building itself, because such items usually have shorter recovery periods (meaning that you can take more of the value—as much as 20 or even 33 percent—each year until the end of the depreciation period).

#224. What kind of business records should I keep?

Your business records for your rental property should be relatively easy to set up and maintain. A file folder for each tenant should be created. All documents and information about each tenant should be retained in the file folder.

Rejected applications should be retained. Be prepared to show why the applicant was denied tenancy. Keep the information that proves why the application was rejected, as well as the denial letter.

Business records should also show all income received, as well as expenses paid to maintain or repair the property. Keep accurate records that include receipts and check payments to verify all necessary and appropriate expenses. These records should be reviewed yearly by your tax preparation professional.

Your records should also include detailed information about the cost of acquiring the property, capital improvements, and depreciation claimed on your annual taxes.

#225. What business expenses am I permitted to deduct?

All legitimate business expenses are lawful deductions from your income. Direct expenses are easily identified and obviously deductible. Some examples include:

- Repairs made to an appliance in a rental unit
- Advertising that a rental unit is available

- Purchase price of a smoke detector for a rental unit
- Legal costs for advice and consultation to operate your rental property

Other deductible costs include automobile expense. Each year, the IRS publishes the amount that can be deducted for each mile driven for direct business purposes. By maintaining proper records that include a mileage log of business trips, landlords are permitted to deduct the costs of using their automobile.

Other obvious and legitimate expenses include monthly telephone services, insurances, cleaning expenses, management fees, costs associated in the operation and maintenance of the rental units, professional services, taxes, and office expenses. Mortgage interest and other financing expenses are deductible. Repairs are also deductible.

#226.   When should I get professional tax help?

All landlords should seek the assistance of a professional to handle their taxes. A professional can suggest ways to reduce the landlord's tax liability legally.

There are many different and legitimate deductions available to property owners that have rental income. There is no reason not to claim every legitimate deduction and expense.

The best time to find and hire a tax professional is any time other than tax season, which runs from January 1 to April 15. Other times of the year are far less busy. Find a tax professional that has experience handling the tax returns of other landlords.

Income tax returns of landlords are often complicated and involved because of complex tax laws and regulations. They should only be completed by proficient and experienced tax consultants and professionals. Lawmakers often make changes to statutes because of political will and events. For example, following the September 11 attacks in New York City, Congress amended the tax laws to make it more favorable to invest there. Only a full-time professional tax consultant could keep up with the annual changes.

#227. **What kind of tax planning should I do?**

Tax planning for landlords is simple and straightforward. Landlords normally make a small profit on their rental income. In many cases, rental income is usually sufficient to pay a mortgage, taxes, insurance, and repairs. There is usually a small amount of money left over for the other expenses. However, landlords are permitted to depreciate the purchase price of the rental property, which is usually sufficient to turn a small economic profit into a small tax loss. That results in the expenses exceeding income after depreciation is taken into consideration. The IRS tax rules provide a legitimate tax break for property owners that rent their property instead of using it as a personal residence.

Certain years, landlords face major expenses, such as replacing a roof or remodeling a rental unit after a long-term tenant vacates the property. In these circumstances, it is possible that the landlord has a loss greater than $25,000. But the IRS Passive Activity Loss rules will limit the loss to exactly $25,000. The remainder can be carried over to the next year, when the landlord will hopefully earn more of a profit on the property and will be able to absorb the excessive tax losses from the previous year.

#228. **What is a repair reserve?**

A repair reserve is a cash fund established by a landlord. The money is kept in a separate account, much like a savings account, and is used only when major repairs or renovations are needed to the property.

Successful landlords often deposit a preset amount in the fund each month. It is essentially a savings account to be used for such things as roof replacement, plumbing repairs, or capital improvements, such as replacing the heating and cooling system.

The amount budgeted to be saved each month is often determined by the age of the building, and what the landlord believes future repairs and replacements may be each year. If the landlord believes $3,600 should be budgeted for the repair reserve, then $300 a month is deposited into this account.

The repair reserve is certainly nothing more than an educated guess as to what might be needed over the coming months. As time passes, it becomes easier to determine accurately what amount of money should be held in a repair reserve.

#229. What is a vacancy reserve?

A vacancy reserve is a fund that a landlord sets up to handle those months when rent is not received. The vacancy reserve is used in those months when the property is vacant during tenant turnovers or when the current tenant does not pay rent.

Successful landlords must have a substantial amount of money in reserve so that they can both cover the mortgage in the event they have vacancies and to cover any projected and unexpected repairs. Without a vacancy reserve, a landlord is often tempted to reduce the standards of an applicant.

The amount of the cash reserve should probably and ideally be about the equivalent of three to four months of rental income. It is not easy for many to build that much of a cash reserve, but it should be a goal and part of your financial planning.

#230. Can the security deposit be increased?

In some areas, laws or regulations control the amount of the security deposit. Generally, when controls are in place, the total amount of the security deposit cannot be more than the equivalent of two months' rent for an unfurnished rental unit. Furnished residential rental units cannot have a security deposit greater than three months' rent.

Security deposits generally cannot be raised during the rental period. Many areas have established laws that prohibit any increases. Many landlords collect the equivalent of one month's rent as a security deposit. When the rent increases, the landlord also asks for an additional security deposit. In some areas, this may not be allowed.

The lease agreement will state whether the security deposit can be increased during the term of occupancy. When the term is completed (for example, after twelve months of a one-year leasing agreement), the rent and security deposit can be renegotiated. With a month-to-month rental, the security deposit can be legally increased every thirty days.

Many successful landlords keep the security deposit set slightly less than the equivalent of one month's rent. By doing so, it eliminates the tenant claiming or requesting that the security deposit be used as the last month's rent payment.

#231. **What notices must I give my tenant?**

The lease agreement often specifies how notices must be given from the landlord to the tenant. Many of the required notices are for entry to perform repairs or maintenance. Other provisions for notices pertain to notification for changes in rent, terms of the lease, or other similar notifications.

The landlord should give a minimum of twenty-four hours notice for nonemergency entrance into the tenant's rented space. The advance notice should always be in writing. For those landlords that overlook this notification, penalties could include claims of invasion of privacy or unlawful trespass.

Even if the landlord is not the one actually entering the property, but rather a vendor (such as an employee of a pest control company), the landlord could be held responsible. This is why it is always best to place all notifications in writing.

#232. **How do I find reliable contractors?**

One of the best sources of contractors is referrals and recommendations of others. This is always the best way. A referral by a satisfied customer should always be a good indication of who to use for work at your property.

Always ask people you know who have hired contractors and ask questions about quality of work, pricing, and communication skills. Even if you do not have any immediate needs, find out who completed good work. Always ask if there were any surprises, pleasant or otherwise.

You can also often check with local government or landlord associations for contractor referrals. Be aware that referrals from these kinds of sources may be affected by politics and friendships and may not necessarily point you towards the best work.

Any contractor you hire should carry liability insurance. In some areas, contractors may also have licenses, but often a license means nothing in terms of providing you with any assurances about the quality of a given contractor's work.

#233. **When should I use a handyman service instead of a contractor?**

It depends on the work that needs to be completed at your property. Most successful landlords use a handyman service for small jobs. Contractors often taken on the larger, more complicated tasks.

Handyman services vary. They often include the small jobs that other companies won't do, or are just too expensive. For example, if just one roof shingle needs to be replaced, a handyman service is likely to get the job done faster and less expensively than a roofing contractor.

Some handyman services are simply entrepreneurs that carry various tools and hardware in a truck, ready to do all kinds of work at a moment's notice. From light carpentry to the installation of appliances, the types of tasks a handyman service can do are nearly unlimited. Such services are often needed by a landlord.

What tasks a handyman service can and will do vary from one area to the next. The experience of the handyman service in addition to local licensure requirements determines what work you can get completed.

#234. Is there anything I can do to pay less for utilities?

There are some things a landlord can do to reduce the costs of utilities. These include purchasing low energy appliances, installing timers, and adding insulation.

In many areas, weatherization programs exist that help property owners reduce energy costs. Some programs are grants that you do not have to repay.

In some areas, there are different utility companies that offer competitive rates. Changes in laws require one utility to make their service lines available to other companies. By rate shopping and selecting a different company, the landlord can reduce the cost of the utilities.

Installing meters can allow the landlord to require the tenants to pay for metered utilities, such as gas, water, and electricity. By passing the costs on to the tenant, the landlord does not have to pay for wasted or careless use of utilities. Tenants that must pay for the utilities are less likely to leave lights on unnecessarily or waste water usage.

#235. Are property taxes ever negotiable?

Once the property tax bill is received from the tax collector, the only thing to do is to pay it. Most tax bills allow for some small discount by paying early. The discount is often between 1 and 2 percent.

Some lenders pay the tax bills from escrowed funds. Each month, the lender requires the property owner to pay one-twelfth of the projected tax bill into an escrowed account. When the tax bill is issued, it is paid from this account. Always submit the tax bill promptly to get the discount.

The time to negotiate a property tax is after the assessment. There is always some form of appeal to any property tax assessment. You do not need to be a lawyer or hire one to appeal a property tax assessment. Simply prepare evidence (other nearby property sales, current market listings, and other assessed properties similar to yours) and appear at a hearing or the appeals board. You will need to testify what you believe the value of your property is and submit your evidence.

#236. **What fixed costs can be reduced?**

One of the best things you can do is to avoid unnecessary costs. For example, suppose you could save $5,000 a year in expenses. Saving $5,000 in fixed costs is the same as an equal increase in income. You have $5,000 more in your pocket. A landlord took two hours to shop for property insurance. By doing so, he saved $100 a year. He could have accepted the first quote and been done with his search for insurance. Instead, he persevered and found the same insurance for $100 less than his first quote. Another way to look at this is to say he earned $50 an hour. That isn't a bad return on two hours worth of time.

Always look for ways that can reduce your fixed costs. From less expensive financing to shopping for heating oil and insurance, always seek price quotes and be willing to switch vendors for better service and lower prices. Maintenance always makes sense. It reduces the necessity of expensive repairs later. Keep your property in excellent condition.

#237. **What regular adjustable costs can be reduced?**

For nonemergency repairs or jobs that are needed at your property, always seek competitive bids from contractors. Although this isn't necessary for smaller jobs (less than $100 and usually completed by your handyman service), it is important for larger jobs and will help lower your costs.

Make the rental unit more energy efficient. Roll out or blow in insulation. Wrap the pipes. Caulk windows and door jams. Eliminate leaks that allow heat or cooling to escape. Making the unit more energy efficient reduces the power bills.

Look for ways to reduce water consumption. From low volume water usage toilets to new showerheads, there are many ways you can reduce your rental unit's water consumption. By doing so, you may also reduce your sewer service bill, as in many locales that is determined by water usage.

Review your service contracts. You may want to pay per service rather than per month. For example, your exterior maintenance company may only charge you each time they mow the yard or shovel snow. It may be less expensive to pay as you go. Or it might be cheaper to contract for a year, without paying each time the company provides service.

#238. **What is the difference between renting and leasing?**

In some jurisdictions, there could be a significant legal difference, and in others, it means the same thing.

Often the terms "renting" and "leasing" are used interchangeably. Technically, renting is when you pay money for the use of a property but never gain anything other than the use and occupancy during the rental term. Leasing often implies that a part of your money could be used to acquire ownership and affords occupancy or use during the lease period.

But the terms, through common usage, have been muddied. In some areas, renting means thirty days or less, while leasing means the equivalent of renting for more than thirty days, and is typically a term of six months to one year. Renting is often less formal. For example, you might rent a chair and umbrella at a beach—the period of the rental is just a few hours. You are still under the obligation to return the owner's property when the rental is concluded.

Leasing always requires the execution of a written agreement. Renting does not require a written agreement, but for the protection of both the tenant and the landlord, it should.

#239. What should I do when a tenant pays for a repair without authorization, and then reduces the rent payment for that amount of the repair?

The first consideration is to determine if the repair was legitimate, necessary, and reasonable. Some repairs are. When they are, honor the payment made by the tenant, and reimburse the costs. Often a friendly letter that includes a thank you can go a long way to maintain good will with the tenant.

For example, if the tenant replaces the hose from the pipe that feeds the clothes washer, and submits a twenty dollar receipt from a local home improvement center, accept it. It would cost more than the cost of the hose if water damage occurred. Also, your handyman (or you) would have had to replace the hose, costing additional time and money.

#240. When is it best to sell my rental property?

There are any number of reasons why you may want to sell your rental property. One of the primary reasons many landlords sell their rental property is to get out of the landlord business.

Perhaps it is best described as "burnout," but that may be one reason why a rental income property is sold. A sure sign of burnout is when you do not want to answer the phone because it might be another call from a tenant. When you don't enjoy owning the property any longer, it is time to sell it.

Other valid reasons to sell include:

- Major repairs will be needed soon to the property, and you do not have the desire to oversee those repairs being made.
- Managing the building is just taking too much of your time.
- The neighborhood is deteriorating.
- You are becoming more lax in maintaining the property, probably because it has become a burden to you.
- You no longer want the responsibility of owning the property.
- You want your money out of the property.

#241. **What is a 1031 exchange?**

A 1031 exchange, also commonly known as a tax-deferred exchange, is a simple strategy and method for selling one property and then proceeding with an acquisition of another property within a specific period. The designation 1031 relates to the IRS tax code. Both properties must be qualified, as defined by the IRS rules.

The logistics and process of selling a property and then buying another property are practically identical to any standardized sale and buying situation. However, a 1031 exchange is unique because the entire transaction is treated as an exchange and not just as a simple sale. It is this difference between "exchanging" and not simply buying and selling which allows the taxpayer to qualify for a deferred gain treatment. In simple terms, sales of real estate are taxable with the IRS, while 1031 exchanges are not.

Before proceeding with any 1031 exchange, make sure you understand the mechanics and how this works. Consult with both your attorney and your tax professional to make sure you know how to comply fully with the IRS regulations.

#242.   When should I consider a 1031 exchange?

A 1031 exchange makes sense to avoid legally tax liability that you would owe to the IRS. The 1031 exchange can be complicated. There are strict timelines involved with the exchange. For example, to qualify, you must complete the exchange within 180 days.

A person who has sold the relinquished property must receive the replacement property within this period. It is referred to as the Exchange Period under the 1031 exchange rule. According to the 1031 exchange rule published by the IRS, the 180-day timeline has to be adhered to under all circumstances. It is not extendable in any situation, even if the 180th day falls on a Saturday, Sunday, or legal holiday.

The foundation of the 1031 exchange rule is that the properties involved in the transaction must be "like kind" and both properties must be held for a productive purpose in business or trade, as an investment.

Because of the intricacies of the tax code and IRS rules governing a 1031 exchange, always consult with both your tax professional and attorney to understand fully your obligations and liabilities.

#243.   How often should I raise the rent?

Raising the rent can cause a lot of anxiety and concern for a landlord. It is never an easy decision.

From the landlord's viewpoint, the rent should be raised annually. Unless the lease prohibits or there are local ordinances that prohibit or limit rent increases, the rent should be raised annually. Raising the rent often means an increase of 3 to 5 percent—it could be more or less. Since rent is the source of income on the property, the more that can be collected, the more money you should make by increasing the amount your tenant pays for occupancy.

Of course, nothing is more likely to make your tenant move than increasing the rent. Many tenants will emotionally respond to the rent increase, even though it might be quite reasonable or cost them more to move than to pay the increased amount.

Rent should be reviewed each year of tenancy and should be raised when appropriate. Always keep an eye on what other similar rental units cost in the same neighborhood as your property.

#244. How much notice should I give my tenant when I plan to raise the rent?

At a minimum, you should give forty-five days. Most jurisdictions will require the notification to be at least thirty days. The language of your lease, as well as local laws, may require a longer notification before the rent can be raised.

Raising the rent may mean the loss of the tenant. If you can rent the unit quickly for more than the current tenant is willing to pay, then it usually makes sense to raise the rent. If the tenant decides to move, so be it. Either way, you will receive more rent for the property.

Always put the rent increase in writing. Include a place on the form or letter for the tenant to accept the rent increase, and ask for it to be returned to you within a short time.

Don't raise the rent verbally. The tenant may try to continue to pay the old rent, ignoring your increase. Without the written notice, it will be difficult to prove that you did raise the rent when you begin the eviction process.

#245. **What should I consider before I raise the rent?**

Before increasing the rent, make sure that the local housing market will support your higher rental rate. Research other rental properties in your area before making your final decision about raising the rent. If the majority of the other properties are charging less for rent, you probably will not attract new tenants—or even retain your existing tenants.

When interest rates are down, it is often harder to find tenants, because they are buying houses rather than renting. When interest rates increase, people can't afford to purchase a home and will often rent, making the demand for rental housing increase. Everything depends on your local market.

The bottom line is that you need to determine the market for rent before you send out the increase notice. Share with your tenant any recent increases in property taxes, fuel costs, insurance expenses, or any other increases you have had to pay. Share the results of your rent survey in at least a general way, stating that the apartment is still priced at or below the competition.

#246. **Is there anything I can do to help retain my tenants when I raise the rent?**

Think of the rent increase notice as a sales letter. This letter should never be a sterile recitation of the facts surrounding the increase.

Instead, your sales pitch should be a reminder of all the great things you have done around the property in the last year, the great service that you have rendered, the late fees that you forgave, the prompt repairs or improvements that you made inside of the tenant's unit, and anything else you can possibly think of to justify the rent increase.

Use proper language to sell the new rent. Don't describe the increase as an increase of rent, but rather explain it is an adjustment or a change. If the change in rent can be correctly expressed as an adjustment of just a percentage point or two, say so. Sometimes it is helpful to break down the adjustment in terms of the cost per day instead of the cost per month. An adjustment of $25 per month is less than one dollar per day. Ask the tenant if he is really going to move over less than one dollar per day?

#247. What are government-mandated repairs and improvements?

The government may mandate certain repairs or improvements to your property. The list of what they might want you to do is long and varied, and often depends on your location. You could be required to connect to a public sewage or water system, install or repair sidewalks, or comply with landscape restrictions.

You cannot ignore such notices from the local authorities. Usually there is a window of opportunity to complete the work. If, at the end of that time, you have not made the mandated repairs or improvements, legal action can be commenced against you.

Many municipalities have annual inspections of elevators, boilers, and other complicated equipment that might discover a need for a repair that many laymen landlords may not have realized. When a local official, such as a building inspector, requires that certain repairs be made, realize that you have little negotiating leverage.

#248. Should I offer a tenant a lease purchase option?

If you are going to offer your tenant a lease purchase option, make sure your tenant understands what a lease option is, and be sure your tenant is able to qualify for a loan from a legitimate lender.

You and your lease purchase option tenant should schedule a meeting with your lender to determine the viability of your lease purchase option program. The lender will be able to coach your tenant on what they may need to do to clear up their credit or otherwise prepare to take out a mortgage in the future.

It is grossly unfair to take a renter's money for a purchase option knowing that they will never be able to qualify for a mortgage. Do not use a lease purchase option as a way to rent a marginal property. Use this only as a way to sell a property to a tenant that needs help to purchase their first property.

#249. What happens to the tenants when a landlord sells the building?

Nothing. The terms and conditions of the rental agreement must be honored by the new property owner.

The tenant cannot be evicted without cause. The sale of a property is not cause for eviction unless there's a clause in the lease permitting the landlord to terminate the lease upon selling the property. Lease agreements require action from both the landlord and the tenant. It requires the tenant to pay rent for the lease period, and it requires the landlord to rent the unit for the lease period. Neither party can break this agreement without consent or a clause written into the lease.

Laws may vary by state. New owners may terminate a lease after ninety or 120 days notice, and usually must pay relocation expenses for the tenant.

The new owner may want the tenant to sign a new lease. The tenant does not need to do so unless it is advantageous to do so.

#250. Can I have a coin-operated laundry in my rental property?

If your investment property has four units or more, it usually makes sense to provide coin-operated laundry appliances. You can buy, install, and maintain the machines yourself, or you can retain a service provider.

If you decide to retain a contractor, be sure to work with a reputable firm, as there are so many opportunities for you to be shorted on the revenue.

Most coin laundry leases allow for a fifty-fifty split of revenue between you and the contractor. You are responsible for providing the room and the utilities for the machines, and the contractor provides the equipment and any needed service, including collecting the coins.

To induce a contractor to install new equipment in your building, you will probably need to make at least a three-year commitment, allowing the vendor exclusive rights to operate the coin concession. These service agreements are notorious for having automatic renewal clauses that are difficult to avoid or cancel. Insist after the initial period (of hopefully no more than three years) that the agreement becomes month to month with cancellation possible at any time.

SAMPLE LETTERS

Approval of Applicant

November 17, 2009
Fred and Wilma Mercer
989 West North Street
Jeffers, PA 18998

Dear Fred and Wilma:

I am pleased to inform you that your application for the rental of 115 South East Road, Jeffers, has been approved.

Your monthly rent will be $900. As we both agreed, there will no pets permitted on the property, which entitles you to a reduced security deposit of $750.

Tenancy will begin, as you requested, on November 28. There will be no charge for rent for November 28, 29, or 30.

Please call me at 717-555-1255 to set a time to sign the lease.

We will hold this rental for you until November 24. If the lease is not signed by that date, we will assume you are no longer interested and will offer it to the next approved applicant.

I am sure you will enjoy living in the property.

Looking forward to meeting with you.

Sincerely,

Frederica J. Johns
9 Trapped Road
Jeffers, PA 18998

Denial of Application

November 17, 2009
Fred and Wilma Mercer
989 West North Street
Jeffers, PA 18998

Dear Fred and Wilma:

I am sorry to inform you that your application for the rental of 115 South East Road, Jeffers, has been declined.

We require monthly income four times the amount of the rent. The monthly rent for the unit is $900, requiring a minimum monthly income of $3,600. We were only able to verify your monthly income to be $3,085. Unfortunately, your current income is not sufficient to qualify.

Thank you for your interest in the property.

Sincerely,

Frederica J. Johns
9 Trapped Road
Jeffers, PA 18998

THE 250 QUESTIONS

Part One: Ideal (And Not So Ideal) Properties

1:   What are some of the risks of being a landlord?

2:   Is being a landlord a good financial strategy?

3:   Can I really make money as a landlord?

4:   Is there really a demand for rental properties?

5:   Is being a landlord difficult?

6:   How much work is involved in owning properties?

7:   What are some of the common problems many landlords experience?

8:   What is the best type of property to use for rental income?

9:   How much should I pay for a rental property?

10:   Are there any types of properties that I should avoid?

11:   What is the most I should pay for a rental property?

12:   Do fixer-uppers make the best rental investment properties?

13:   How do I find good rental properties?

14:   Do starter properties make better rental properties?

15:   Should I buy properties that are already being used as rental properties?

16:   How much should I spend to convert a property to one that produces rental income?

17:   How do I know a good deal when I see it?

18:   Are multiple-family properties a better investment than single-family properties?

19:   Are two-family properties better or worse than three- or four-unit properties?

20:   What are some of the financing options for acquiring rental investment properties?

21:   How much money do I need for a down payment?

45:   Am I required to have fire extinguishers in the rental property?

46:   What kind of locks must be on the doors?

47:   Are there other security safeguards that I must provide?

48:   What appliances must I provide?

49:   Must I provide communication connectivity, such as cable TV, telephone, or television antennas?

50:   How should I handle the exterior maintenance of the property?

51:   What should I do about common access areas?

Part Two: Finding and Screening Tenants

52:   What are the best ways to find tenants?

53:   Should I advertise for tenants?

54:   Should I use a real estate agent to find tenants?

55:   Is it safer to rent to a friend or relative than a stranger?

56:   What is the correct way to show a property to a prospective tenant?

57:   How can I legally screen a tenant?

58:   What should I ask a prospective tenant?

59:   What kind of application form should I use?

60:   Who should complete the application?

61:   May I charge an application fee?

62:   Can I restrict prospective tenants from having specific possessions, such as motorcycles or waterbeds?

63:   Is a first come, first served policy legal and effective?

64:   What selection criteria should I follow?

65:   How can I verify employment?

66:   During the screening process, what should I be looking for?

67: How much time do I have to screen an applicant?

68: Can I use a minimum income requirement to screen tenants?

69: What is the best way to verify a prospective tenant's income?

70: How can I check a prospective tenant's credit?

71: May I charge a fee for a credit check?

72: What should I look for on a credit report?

73: Should I rent to someone with perfect rental history but poor consumer credit?

74: Should I ask for references?

75: What am I allowed to ask a reference about a prospective tenant?

76: What questions am I allowed to ask a tenant?

77: What questions am I not allowed to ask a tenant?

78: What is steering?

79: Does HUD really enforce the Fair Housing and Equal Housing Opportunity Laws on small-business landlords?

80: Should I contact current or past landlords?

81: What can I ask a current or past landlord about the prospective tenant?

82: What is a tenant screening service?

83: Am I allowed to ask for identification from a prospective tenant?

84: How do I reject an applicant?

85: How do I accept an applicant?

86: How long should approved applicants have to accept my offer of renting the property to them?

87: Do I need to use a written lease?

88: What should be included in a lease?

89: Should I rent a property for a one-year period?

90: When does a month-to-month rental make sense?

91: Where can I get a blank lease to use?

92: Should I require that my tenant purchase tenants' insurance?

93: What is the difference between a Certificate of Insurance and an Additional Named Insured document from a property insurer?

94: When do I collect the security deposit?

95: What is the maximum amount of security deposit I can impose?

96: Are there any special restrictions on how I handle the tenant's security deposit?

97: What creative methods can I use to market my property?

98: Should I offer incentives to attract better tenants?

99: How should I structure a rent-to-own deal?

100: What is the difference between a lease purchase or option-to-buy versus a rent-to-own transaction?

101: Which utilities should I pay?

102: What utilities should I require the tenant to pay?

103: Should I ever give my tenants "free rent" as part of their move-in?

Part Three: Managing the Property

104: What is a move-in inspection?

105: How should a move-in inspection be conducted?

106: What is a tenant orientation?

107: Can I restrict smoking in my rental unit?

108: Am I allowed to have a "no pets" policy?

109: Am I permitted to have a no children policy?

110: Can I limit the number of people that may live in the property?

111: What is the best way to collect the rent?

112: What should I do when a rent payment is late?

113: How much tolerance should I give a late-paying renter?

114: Am I allowed to collect late fees on past due rent?

115: Should I accept partial payments of the rent that is due?

116: Where can a landlord get help with rent collection?

117: Are there any creative ways to get the rent paid on time?

118: Should I keep a copy of all rent checks received from a tenant?

119: Am I allowed to charge a fee for a bad or insufficient funds check given to me by a tenant for rent?

120: What should a landlord do if a tenant declares bankruptcy?

121: Can I raise the rent during the lease period?

122: How often can a landlord raise the rent?

123: What is the most common reason landlords do not start the eviction process?

124: What are the standard rules for tenants?

125: Should the tenant rules be made part of the lease?

126: How should scheduled or routine maintenance be completed?

127: When can a landlord enter a rental unit?

128: Can a tenant give permission to enter the rental unit?

129: What are the best ways to handle emergency repairs?

130: Should I charge for accidental lockouts?

131: If a tenant pays the rent but breaks the rules, can the tenant be evicted?

132: Can tenants drill holes to install electronics and other similar items?

133: How should I plan and handle major repairs or renovations?

134: What should I do when repairs do not go as planned?

135: Should I ever allow my tenants to do repairs or renovations?

136: Is it wise to allow tenants to paint the rental unit?

137: Does it make sense to expect or require a tenant to perform maintenance work, like grass cutting and snow removal, as part of the rental agreement?

138: What is the best way to handle appliance problems?

139: What should I do about moisture problems?

140: How do I comply with the lead paint disclosure?

141: What do you do when a tenant simply abandons the property?

142: When does a tenant lose ownership of personal property left at a rental property?

143: When the tenant abandons the rental unit, what should the landlord do with the property the tenant has left on the premises?

144: What should I do if the tenant's Notice of Abandonment is returned to me?

145: Should I spend time and money to track down a tenant that has skipped and still owes rent?

146: Can I evict a tenant for something other than nonpayment of rent?

147: What should I do when a tenant violates a no-pets policy?

148: What is the eviction process?

149: What is "normal wear and tear"?

150: Can I charge a tenant by deducting it from the security deposit for leaving trash, dirt, and filth in the rental unit?

151: How do I calculate tenant-caused damages?

152: How do I calculate cleanup costs?

153: How do I withhold part of the security deposit for damages?

154: How long do I have to refund all or part of the security deposit?

155: When does it make sense to hire a property manager?

156: How much does a property manager cost?

157: What can I do to make my property more attractive to prospective tenants?

158: What should I do about keeping the outside of the property maintained?

Part Four: Legal Issues

159: What federal laws must I know?

160: What state laws must I know?

161: What local municipality laws must I know?

162: Are there any local health codes that I need to know?

163: How do I keep up with the changes in laws and regulations?

164: What is rent control?

165: What is a Section 8 rental?

166: Is seeking a Section 8 tenant a good strategy?

167: Are there advantages to having a Section 8 rental property?

168: Is it legal to rent a property with black mold?

169: If a tenant claims a property has mold, can they break the lease?

170: If a fire or some other disaster makes the unit uninhabitable, what are my responsibilities to the tenant?

171: Can a landlord be held responsible for crime against a tenant?

172: What can I legally require of my tenant?

173: How can a landlord protect their properties from criminals?

174: Can a landlord require the tenant to sign written agreements?

175: What can I do if a tenant wants to break the lease and move?

176: Why should I allow a tenant to break a lease?

177: What is mitigation?

178: Is the landlord ever permitted to break a lease?

179: How does a landlord legally evict a tenant?

180: If there is no written lease, how do I initiate an eviction?

181: What rights does the tenant have if a landlord refuses to make repairs?

182: When can a tenant sublet a rental unit?

183: What can a landlord do when a tenant sublets a property without permission to do so?

184: Can a landlord evict a tenant for selling drugs or gang activity?

185: Is a landlord permitted to evict a tenant during the winter?

186: Does a tenant that is elderly, disabled, or pregnant have any special rights?

187: How can a landlord avoid the eviction process?

188: Should a landlord ever be lenient with a late-paying tenant?

189: How long does a landlord have to start a court action against a tenant?

190: How long does a tenant have to start a court action against the landlord?

191: Should a landlord avoid small claims court?

192: Is a landlord responsible for a defective appliance?

193: What is a rent escalator clause?

194: When should a landlord call the police about a tenant?

195: Can a landlord pester a tenant until they leave the property?

196: Should I accept the rent after I file an eviction notice with the court?

197: Can I proceed with eviction even if the rent is paid by the tenant?

198: What should I do when the tenant vacates the property?

199: What kind of inspection should I do when the property is vacated?

Part Five: Controlling Expenses

200: Should I pay for trash removal?

201: How can I be sure the tenant pays for the trash, gas, water, or sewer bills?

202: What kinds of insurance do I need?

203: What is tenant relocation insurance?

204: What is rent loss insurance?

205: Do I need flood insurance?

206: What type of liability insurance do I need?

207: What type of property coverage insurance should I purchase?

208: How much insurance is enough?

209: What kind of financing should I seek for rental property purchases?

210: Should I ever pay financing points?

211: Is it better to use a bank or a mortgage company for rental property financing?

212: What are some ways to pay less for financing?

213: When should I refinance my rental property?

214: What should I consider when setting an operating budget?

215:   What is the life expectancy of appliances?

216:   How can I save money on appliances?

217:   Can I require a tenant to clean the rental unit when they move?

218:   What type of maintenance should I routinely schedule?

219:   Should I do my own repairs?

220:   What repairs are tenants responsible for paying?

221:   How do I maximize my tax deductions?

222:   What do I need to know about the IRS Schedule E?

223:   What amount can I claim as depreciation?

224:   What kind of business records should I keep?

225:   What business expenses am I permitted to deduct?

226:   When should I get professional tax help?

227:   What kind of tax planning should I do?

228:   What is a repair reserve?

229:   What is a vacancy reserve?

230:   Can the security deposit be increased?

231:   What notices must I give my tenant?

232:   How do I find reliable contractors?

233:   When should I use a handyman service instead of a contractor?

234:   Is there anything I can do to pay less for utilities?

235:   Are property taxes ever negotiable?

236:   What fixed costs can be reduced?

237:   What regular adjustable costs can be reduced?

238:   What is the difference between renting and leasing?

239:   What should I do when a tenant pays for a repair without authorization, and then reduces the rent payment for that amount of the repair?

240:   When is it best to sell my rental property?

241:   What is a 1031 exchange?

242:   When should I consider a 1031 exchange?

243:   How often should I raise the rent?

244:   How much notice should I give my tenant when I plan to raise the rent?

245:   What should I consider before I raise the rent?

246:   Is there anything I can do to help retain my tenants when I raise the rent?

247:   What are government-mandated repairs and improvements?

248:   Should I offer a tenant a lease purchase option?

249:   What happens to the tenants when a landlord sells the building?

250:   Can I have a coin-operated laundry in my rental property?

Index